MOTORCYCLE
COLOR · HISTORY

Indian Scout

Jerry Hatfield

MBI Publishing Company

First published in 2001 by MBI Publishing
Company, Galtier Plaza, Suite 200,
380 Jackson Street, St. Paul, MN 55101-3885 USA

MBI Publishing Company books are also
available at discounts in bulk quantity for
industrial or sales-promotional use. For details
write to Special Sales Manager at Motorbooks
International Wholesalers & Distributors
Galtier Plaza, Suite 200, 380 Jackson Street,
St. Paul, MN 55101-3885 USA

Hatfield, Jerry
    Indian Scout/Jerry Hatfield
        p. cm.— (Motorcycle Color History)
    Includes index.
    ISBN 0-7603-0813-6 (pbk. : alk. paper)
    1. Indian Motorcycle—History.
    I. Title II. Motorbooks International
        motorcycle color history.
TL448.I4 H38 2001
629.227'5—dc21   2001-030748

On the front cover: The 1927 Scout was pivotal. From 1920 through 1926, the 600-cc Scout was renowned for its ease of handling, rugged reliability, and ample power for the mostly dirt roads of the era. For the 1927 season, Indian enlarged the engine to 750 cc. The power increase exceeded the 25-percent-capacity growth and transformed the Scout from a practical motorcycle to a bike that could fill all roles, from beginner's bike to champion racer.

On the frontispiece: The 1920 Scout was right on target with its compact, user-friendly layout. The Scout's 55- miles-per-hour top speed was seldom seen because of the era's poor roads.

On the title page: This 1920 Scout was restored in Spain. In 1920, Indian was the world's largest motorcycle manufacturer. The iron redskins sold well in foreign markets because they were designed for dirt roads whereas British and European bikes were designed for pavement. Scene from within Leon Cathedral, Leon, Spain, by permission of Father Manuel Perez-Recio. Photography by Eduardo Gonzalez-Puras. Project management of all church-related pictures: Enrique Castells Fernandez.

On the back cover: In 1948 the oldest continuous rivalry in motorsports was Indian versus Harley-Davidson. The iron redskins went out in a blaze of glory with a final batch of 25 special "Daytona" Scouts. Floyd Emde won the 1948 Daytona 200 on one of these bikes.

Edited by Darwin Holmstrom
Designed by LeAnn Kuhlmann

Printed in China

Contents

Acknowledgments

I am indebted to the Research Center, Henry Ford Museum, and Greenfield Village for the use of the E. Paul du Pont Papers. All du Pont correspondence in this book is cited to "E. Paul du Pont Papers, Research Center, Henry Ford Museum, and Greenfield Village."

To "the Indian men," my thanks for their priceless insights. Jack Armstrong discussed the history of the postwar "Big Base" Sport Scouts, sharing his experiences as a racer along with the recollections of his father, "Pop" Armstrong. Allen Carter recalled his experiences in the factory as a test engineer, described the factory, explained factory operations, and related the history of Model 841 development. Stephen du Pont explained his engineering work with the prewar "Big Base" Sport Scout racers and other Indian engineering matters. Bobby Hill discussed his racing career and provided photos. Matt Keevers described Ralph Rogers. Departed Indian racing stars provided insights, including: Woodsie Catonguay, Jim Davis, Rollie Free, Ed Kretz Sr., and Fred Ludlow. The late Tom Sifton, Harley master tuner, discussed his Indian opponents.

I appreciate my several hosts who also provided photo support. In Australia: Peter and Barbara Arundel, and Warwick and Philipa Ellis; in California: Max and Suzi Bubeck, Bob and Avis Doherty, and Bob and Shorty Stark; in Colorado: Eddie and Elaine Kretz, and Walt and Lucie Timmie; in Connecticut: George and Milli Yarocki; in Massachusetts: Butch and Mary Baer, Malcolm and Dottie Houck; in New Hampshire: Kent and Carol Thompson; in New York: Doug Miller, Tim and Linda Hedden, and Brett Herrey; in North Carolina: Pete and Judy Sink; in Ohio: Chuck and Irene Ewing; in Pennsylvania: Elmer and Jo Lower, and Robin and Kim Markey.

I'm indebted to transatlantic friends for their photo support. In the Netherlands: A. H. S. "Lex" van Essen and photographer Theo Jeukens; in Scotland: Alan Forbes and photographer Robbie Smith; in Spain: Enrique Castells Fernandez, photographer Eduardo Gonzalez-Puras, and Father Manuel Perez-Recio, who granted permission to photograph within the cathedral; in Switzerland and Cypress: Jean-Pierre Muller. I thank Kevin Storey of Australia for his unusual help: driving me and two Scouts to, within, and back from the great Australian Outback.

My thanks to other enthusiasts who assisted in the photography: in Australia: Harry Cutts; in California: Jerry Cordy, Chuck Otis, Jeff Pearson, Jeff Sierck, Brigette van Essen, and Eric Vaughn; in Connecticut: Al Gazza, Will Paley, and Beth and Stephen Podhajecki; in Florida: Newell Wright; in Iowa: Barry Brown, Charles "Chuck" Garrett, and Gordon Rinschler; in Massachusetts: Dean Black, Tom Bresnahann, Patrick Farah, and Randy Walker; in Colorado: Woody Carson; in Ohio: Ken Burian, David Dechambeau, Gary Myers, and Brandon Rowe; in Pennsylvania: Cy Stoner and Al Stroble; in Virginia: Charles Moore. Other assistance was provided by Gene Atkins of Pennsylvania, Bud Bauman of Ohio, Dr. Jerry Schreiber of New Jersey, and Kerry Wright of Texas.

I thank the owners of Indian motorcycles pictured in the book. They and their motorcycles are: 1920 Scout, frontispiece and page 13, Barry Brown; 1920 Scout, title pages (2 and 3), pages 8 and 11, Enrique Castells; 1924 Scout, pages 17 and 18, Peter Arundel; 1926 Scout, page 21, Brett Herrey; 1927 Scout, front cover, pages 22, 24, 25, and 27, Patrick Farah; 1926 hill climber, pages 28 and 29, Peter Arundel; 1929 Series 101 Scout and sidecar, pages 30 and 33, George Yarocki; 1928 Series 101 Scout, page 35; 1930 Series 101 Scout, page 38, Al Gazza; 1930 Series 101 Scout, page 40, Alan Forbes; 1931 Series Scout, page 44, Tom Bresnahan; 1932 "Standard" Scout, pages 48 and 52, Peter Arundel; 1932 Scout Pony, page 48, Robin Markey; 1932 "Standard" Scout, page 51, Jim Dennie; 1934 Sport Scout, pages 46 and 57, Brandon Rowe; 1934 Sport Scout, page 55, Alan

The year 1948 saw Indian relive old glories with a win in America's most pretigious race, the Daytona 200. Winnner Floyd Emde raced a bike identical to this Model 648 Scout except that he used the optional left-hand gear shift and right-hand throttle and his number was 99. Indian built 25 of these special motorcycles and another 25 engines, plus spare parts. These were the last V-twin Scouts that Indian built.

Forbes; 1935 (Standard) Scout, pages 58 and 59, Harry Cutts; 1936 Sport Scout, pages 60, 61, and 62, Peter Arundel; circa-1936 hill climber, page 63, Robin Markey; 1938 Sport Scout, pages 64 and 65, Doug Miller; 1938 Sport Scout, page 67, Malcolm Houck; 1939 Sport Scout racer, page 68, Ed Kretz, Jr.; 1939 Sport Scout, pages 71 and 74, Pete Sink; 1939 Dispatch Tow, pages 72 and 73, Elmer Lower; 1940 Thirty-fifty, pages 76 and 81, Al Stroble; 1940 Sport Scout, page 78, Malcolm Houck; 1940 Sport Scout, page 79, Robin Markey; 1941 Sport Scout, page 82, Elmer Lower; 1941 Sport Scout, page 83, Pete Sink; 1941 Thirty-fifty, page 86, Robin Markey; 1941 Sport Scout, pages 90 and 91, Peter Arundel; Model 741, pages 92 and 96, Robin Markey; Model 640B, page 97, Elmer Lower; Model 841, page 98, Robin Markey; Model 841, page 100, David Dechambeau; 1951 Warrior, pages 104 and 117, Pete Sink; customized Model 741, page 107, Lex van Essen; customized Sport Scout, page 108, David Edwards; Model 648, pages 7, 109, and rear cover, Ken Burian; 1949 Scout, page 110, Pete Sink; 1949 red Arrow, page 112, Bob Stark; 1949 blue Arrow, page 112, Dean Black; 1950 Warrior, page 113, Charles "Chuck" Garrett; Warrior TT, page 114, Chuck Ewing; customized 1949 Scout enduro, pages 118 and 119, Max Bubeck; prototype 1952 Warrior, page 106, Dean Black; 101 Series 101 Scout racer, pages 122 and 123, Eric Vaughn. I'm grateful to the Harley-Davidson Motor Company and to the Harley-Davidson Archives for permission to quote from an official company document. To Morton's Motorcycle Media Ltd., my thanks for copyright release. I thank David Edwards and *Cycle World* for copyright release and their photographer Brian Blades for his photo.

I can't find the words to suitably thank two friends for their special generosity. Peter Arundel funded my Australian adventure. Mary Scholfield donated hundreds of archival photos produced by her late husband, Ken

Chapter One

The Motorcycle for Every Man:
1919–1926

Turn on your imagination. Turn the calendar back to early 1919, and place yourself in Springfield, Massachusetts, a commercial center of the six northeastern states collectively termed "New England." Put yourself in the Indian factory, the famous "Wigwam" of timber frame, brick walls, and external elevator towers, a giant castle-like complex that is the world's largest motorcycle factory. While you're tuning up your imagination, get more specific. It's not enough to be an anonymous worker; make yourself none other than Charles B. Franklin, Indian's leading motorcycle designer.

The Scout ". . . appealed to thousands who heretofore had not been interested in motorcycles, because of its many individual and distinct characteristics. And by the same token, many veteran riders who have felt that the big machines were too heavy welcomed this little masterpiece and were delighted with the opportunities it offered." Source: 1920 Indian sales catalog. Scene from within Leon Cathedral by permission of Father Manuel Perez-Recio. *Eduardo Gonzalez-Puras*

How does American motorcycling look to you, Charlie Franklin—you who came over from your native Ireland three years ago? You who have raced at the Isle of Man, you who is itching to design a trendy new motorcycle better than all the British and continental designs you know so well? How do you see the American motorcycle scene, Charlie Franklin?

First of all, you see your Indian company squirming around, in trouble. It is early 1919 and the Great War has recently ended. For almost two years, your Hendee Manufacturing Company has committed virtually all of Indian motorcycle production to satisfying the needs of American and allied forces. Indian has been patriotic; that's your collective claim. The reality is that patriotism equals profits. Your company has enjoyed its second and third most prosperous years during the war. Quick bucks. Easy bucks. Only one customer; only one price. At the Wigwam, your problem has been simple: to build and build and build. But now your Indian factory returns to a much more complex postwar world. It is a world without guaranteed sales and profits. It is a world with something that Indian hasn't faced before—a rival of equal strength.

The nerve of Harley-Davidson! Sixteen years ago, in 1903, the Milwaukee outfit had been a two-man hobby shop operating in a backyard shed. Never mind that Bill Harley and the Davidson brothers have survived the bloodletting of the infant industry, during which 95 percent of the motorbike builders had gone under. So what? You and your Indian co-workers have always known that some rivals were going to hang around. Now, in 1919, what troubles the front office and you, Charlie Franklin, isn't Harley's survival or even Harley's rapid early growth. And that growth had been rapid. In 1913, Harley-Davidson's 10th year in business, the Milwaukee brand had built about 13,000 machines. In that same year, your Indian Wigwam had rolled out almost triple that number of motorcycles, putting some 32,000 of the iron redskins on the road.

For you, Indian and Charlie Franklin, the problem era is the past two years so recently completed: 1917 and 1918. Your Hendee Manufacturing Company at last realizes it must recapture its lost market lead for Indian motorcycles. Indian, no. 2? Yes. Whammo! In the past two years, while your Wigwam has been building about 42,500 motorcycles for one customer, the Harley-Davidson factory has been building about 45,000 motorcycles for about 30,001 customers—the Army and 30,000 civilians. Equally bad is the dealer situation. There are more Harley dealers in 1919 than in 1916;

there are fewer of your Indian dealers in 1919 than in 1916. This has happened because for about two years your Hendee company had almost no new Indians available for its dealers.

To Build the Better Mousetrap

So, Charlie Franklin, as Indian's chief designer, what do you propose? Your answer: "Let's build a mousetrap."

"Huh?" the reader asks.

"Yes, indeed," Charlie answers, adding, "If you can build a better mousetrap, the world will beat a path unto your door."

That's an old saying which is not quite true—more on that later—but a good place to launch the story. True or not, Indian believes the mousetrap anecdote. Armed with a war chest of profits, backed by a glorious history, sporting the world's best known motorcycle name, a return to former dominance is but a matter of building the better motorcycle. You, Charlie Franklin, will design, and the Wigwam will build, an Indian motorcycle so advanced, so sophisticated, and so superior that it can't be resisted. The new motorcycle will be costly to build, but a breakout into massive sales will yield increased production efficiencies. Thus, superior features will combine with lower cost. The new motorcycle will bring back the glory days of the first decade. The new motorcycle and the old magic of the Indian name will take care of the salesmanship. Dealers will again have an easy time of it, being mainly order takers. Theirs but to keep the motorcycles dry and clean, and to fill out the paperwork of bikes coming and going. Lucky them.

Meanwhile, in the two decades of its life, the American motorcycle industry has lost its focus. Forgotten for so long is the all-important task of first converting prospects into motorcyclists. You, Charlie Franklin, will make the problem clear again, and you will have the answer to the problem.

In 1919 the world's motorcycles are still tied to old ideas about construction. In the old days there were user-friendly machines that resembled the popular pedal bikes, and it had been easy to recruit new "motocycle" riders from the ranks of bicyclists. But by 1919, the friendly bicycle-related pioneer models are all but forgotten, supplanted by ever heavier, bulkier, longer, and higher motorcycles. When a potential convert walks up to a typical 1919 American twin-cylinder model, he learns the saddle is only a couple of inches short of his waistline. The handlebars reach far back like those of a wheelbarrow, to accommodate a rider who sits on the "back row" over the forward tread of the rear tire. If he's 5 foot 9 inches, he can sit on the

saddle and just manage to plant his shoe soles on the ground; any shorter, and it's tippy-toe time. As the potential buyer looks over the typical big American motorcycle, he studies a variety of brackets and clips that, seemingly as afterthoughts, secure the engine and transmission (gearbox) to the single-loop pedal-bike-style frame.

Whether an Indian, a Harley-Davidson, an Excelsior, or the obscure Reading-Standard, the machine appears to be the product of one of those committees that sets out to design a horse but instead produces a camel. It is difficult for the student customer to decide whether the engine and transmission have been compromised to fit

The 1920 Scout engine continued the side-valve (flathead) layout of the 1916–1919 Powerplus big twins but had a new valve operating system. Instead of one central camshaft with two lobes, the Scout had a separate camshaft and lobe for each cylinder. The single cam for each cylinder operated both valves, the cam action being transmitted through a separate lifter for each valve. *Indian sales catalog, George Yarocki collection*

Sectional View of Indian Scout Motor, Type G
HIGHLY EFFICIENT, ECONOMICAL AND SIMPLE
IN CONSTRUCTION

into the frame, or whether the frame is a last-minute accommodation to the powerplant designers who dictate matters at the motorcycle company. Company? One company? To the neophyte, it appears equally possible that the various tacked-together components are built by scattered plants and then merely assembled by the so-called motorcycle manufacturer whose name is on the tank. Although that isn't the case in the United States, motorcycles across the Atlantic are built just that way—and on both sides of the pond the big bikes look largely the same. They are all contraptions first and motorcycles second.

Started from a Blank Sheet

How then, in 1919, to build the first modern postwar American motorcycle? Back to basics. The original small one-cylinder Indians of 1901 through 1908 were integrated designs, meaning that the frame and engine were designed together and by one man. The pioneer Indians had an engine sufficiently small to fit into a heavier version of a conventional pedal-bike frame. The top of the single cylinder was secured directly to the seat mast by a bolt in the center of the cylinder head. The crankcase was secured to the lower frame members.

To achieve this good-looking and good-working result again requires one designer both gifted and empowered. You fit the bill, Charlie Franklin.

You bring to the drawing board the experiences of a factory team rider at the famous Isle of Man TT. You bring to the drawing board your experiences as a team member in the development of America's first big selling side-valve (flathead) motorcycle, the Indian Powerplus, introduced in 1916.

The rest of the "blank sheet" process becomes less clear. So we, the readers, step out of the present tense in 1919, and reflect with hindsight. One is tempted to say that top management gave the designer a blank sheet of paper on which he was to exercise his unfettered genius. But the process may have flowed in the opposite direction. Given that Indian cofounders and genuine motorcyclists George Hendee and Oscar Hedstrom had already left the Wigwam, there could not have been much if any detailed leadership from the company's follow-on-top management team of bankers and financiers. Franklin may have done some sales work within the Wigwam, which means he would have defined some preliminary specifications and made some preliminary drawings in the process of achieving top management's approval for the new "Harley crusher." At any rate, whether before management's blessing and on his own initiative, or after having been charged by management, Franklin really did clear his mind of earlier concepts. Indeed there was a blank sheet of paper—we just don't know when Charles Franklin started filling it in.

Like Syrup over Pancakes

Before drawing the first line on his blank sheet of paper, Charles Franklin first decided that a smaller motorcycle was essential. No more stretching of arms and legs. The success of the 61-ci (1,000-cc) and 74-ci (1,200-cc) Powerplus flatheads of 1916 through 1919 suggested that a smaller engine of the same layout would provide ample power for everyday requirements, especially since the smaller motorcycle would reap the reward of lighter weight. Although there would eventually emerge a new small engine with significantly different internal layout, this was surely a fine-tuning process that came after the new motorcycle concept had first been laid out entirely. Franklin selected an approximate wheelbase, shorter of course. The smaller flathead engine would be low slung, which saved weight by permitting a lower tank and thus a shorter front fork. The shorter distances between the ends of frame tubes gave additional strength, which permitted lighter tubing. This followed the same common-sense logic that one confirms by breaking in two a new pencil, and then breaking one of the pencil halves in two. The shorter the tubes, the stronger the tubes.

What about the frame layout of the new motorcycle? This was probably the first design question, because from the answer came all the other hallmark features of the new motorcycle. By considering the frame first, the rest of the thought process flowed as smoothly as syrup over pancakes. So what useful purpose was served by the current universal use of single-tube main frames in Indians, Harley-Davidsons, Excelsiors, and Reading-Standards? These frames had simply evolved gradually from single-tube pedal-bike frames, in a process that might be termed "design inertia." If instead of a single center-aligned tube, two lower frame tubes were used, one on each side, then the engine and transmission could be firmly anchored between the tubes and enjoy protection in spills. Goodbye bent clips and fractured brackets; hello tidiness. A double-lower-tube frame also meant that footboards could be more securely mounted by fixing them directly to the frame tubes rather than to intermediary fixtures.

Since with a double-lower-tube frame there was no need for an upturned frame tube behind the engine, this awareness must have logically extended to a new possibility: securing the transmission against the back of the engine. The engine, the transmission, and the primary drive housing could be bolted up together into one compact and strong assembly. The temptation to consider a gear-driven primary drive was suddenly upon the designer. If management wouldn't go for the expensive gear-drive layout, at least the drive mechanism could be operated in a cast-aluminum oil bath.

With the realization that the concept was for an integrated "powerplant" rather than a separate engine and transmission came consideration of three-point mounting. As photographers know, any three-legged device always stands firm on the ground. As everyone knows, a four-legged table or chair can wobble around because of unequal-length legs. By mounting the front of the engine to the left and right frame tubes, a single center rear mount can secure the back of the powerplant (the transmission) to a horizontal frame member between the two lower main tubes. Three-point powerplant mounting eliminates any twisting loads on the frame. The major features of the new motorcycle all flowed together, each as a consequence of companion features, to produce one integrated vehicle.

Why Not Overhead Valves?

Your thoughts can be heard: "But what about the engine? Why not overhead valves?" By 1919, Indian Powerplus-based side-valve (flathead or

L-head) racers were out speeding both Indian and Harley-Davidson eight-valve overheads. The Harley eight-valves were the more advanced of the two competing overheads, since they benefited from World War I aviation engineering and thus featured hemispherical combustion chambers and inlet and exhaust valve pairs spread 90 degrees apart. Yet the deceptively simple side-valve Indian racers had more oomph. It was a brief and quirky time in the history of engine development before the advent of tetraethyl lead additives to gasoline (petrol). In opting for flathead engine layout, Indian was simply choosing the engine form that dominated the automobile industry and that on both sides of the Atlantic was winning the premier races.

You ask: "So what about tetraethyl lead? How did its absence promote the flathead engine layout in both motorcycles and cars?" The answer is that in the pre-tetraethyl lead era, fuel simply burned too fast.

Since the beginning of the internal combustion engine field in the late-nineteenth century, it had been appreciated that power was maximized by keeping the initial combustion volume small in relation to the volume opened up by the descending piston (the swept volume). Turning this statement upside-down, power benefited by increasing the ratio of the swept volume to the initial (unswept) volume. With slight modification, this idea becomes the compression ratio, or the ratio of the sum of the swept and unswept volumes divided by the unswept volume.

Among Scout virtues was the cast-aluminum oil bath helical-gear primary drive system. The system was retained in principle right up until the last Indian Chief was built for the 1953 season. Surely among the oldest surviving Scouts is this first-year 1920 model. The motor number, 50R122, means this is the 121st production Scout out of tens of thousands built.

For decades, theoreticians had forecasted cylinder heads with both inlet and exhaust valves upstairs, and with compact combustion chambers that produced high compression ratios. Separating theory from practice was the lack of a fuel that would burn smoothly in a compact overhead-valve cylinder head. Explosion is simply very rapid burning. What happens in a combustion chamber is analogous to a forest fire. Once a forest fire becomes sufficiently hot, fire will break out ahead of the flame front, and trees untouched by the advancing fire will nevertheless burst into flames. The air itself has become so hot that it ignites all ahead of it. Likewise, in a combustion chamber there is an expanding sphere of explosive burning. As in a forest fire, this is termed the flame front. Outside or ahead of the combustion chamber flame front, the as-yet-unburned fuel/air mixture is being rapidly compressed, and with this rapid compression comes a rapid temperature climb, a heat "spike." Thus, "forest fires" start ahead of the flame front, and the one big explosion starts bumping into one or more smaller explosions. In common terms, this uncontrolled explosive burning is variously called "knock," "detonation," or "pre-ignition," according to sub-level details that aren't important enough to this story to explain.

What is important is that without a suitable fuel a typical road-going overhead-valve engine of 1919 produced only a little more power than the counterpart flathead engine. Both engine types were limited in the sense that neither operated reliably (no knocking) with more than about a six-to-one compression ratio. In racing applications, as proven by Indian, the complexities of flow dynamics could completely level the playing field or even work to the advantage of the flathead.

In short, in 1919 the selection of the flathead engine layout was not a compromise in any real sense of the term. Quite the opposite. Indian opted for the world standard, achieving in addition to competitive power the several advantages of a flathead as compared to an overhead-valve or F-head (inlet over exhaust or i.o.e.) engine. The beauty of the flathead was the enclosure of all the vital working parts. Contemporary overhead-valve and F-head engines included, respectively, the open-air exposure of the rocker arms that operated either all or half of the valves. This was thought necessary to promote cooling of the problematic rocker mechanisms, which were further treated to frequent squirt can lubrication. Frequent adjustments were also required on overhead-valve and F-head engines, this being necessary because the oil-covered exposed moving parts captured dirt that worked very effectively as a grinding compound. Meanwhile, oil mist came up through the valve guides and settled all over the engine. Superimposed over this oily mess was a lot of racket, as rockers bounced back and forth. In contrast, flathead engines were more reliable, cleaner, and quieter.

Scouts have always been popular with carnival "Wall of Death" riders. Lightweight and easy handling, plus big motorcycle Vee-twin sound, made—and make—them ideal. Although this picture dates from the mid-1920s, the twenty-first century finds these ancient warriors still in use in carnivals throughout the world. *Baer family collection*

In summary, while theories were out there looking for help (and ultimately finding it), in 1919 it was the real world that mattered. The Scout flathead engine met contemporary real world problems head on—and solved them. The Scout engine was state-of-the-art stuff.

All very simple, very straightforward, and irrefutably logical. Once Franklin's mind was in the proper "gear," it may have taken him no longer to conceive these features than it has taken you to read about them. Strange it is, how one of the hallmarks of genius is to discover the "obvious" when all others have failed to do so.

The rest of the design story was in the details, the details, the details. Trial-and-error dimensions, new engine ideas, cost analyses, budgets, schedules, endless management meetings, work-arounds, and a few hundred drawings, all done in an era of 60-hour work weeks. That's without overtime, so workers really appreciated Saturday afternoons off. Patterns were made, and then a few castings, while the first frame or two went together. Lots of machine shop work tidied up the loose ends, while Franklin's notebooks recorded what didn't quite fit what and why, so that drawings could be revised as necessary.

Hard Metal

Finally, in the summer of 1919 the new motorcycle emerged. The winning strategy, the "better mousetrap"—the bike that stretched the state of the art, was no longer an idea; it was a reality in hard metal. By now, there was a name: "Indian Scout." Ahead were decades of glory to be won under the Scout banner. Motor number 50R000 was stamped to the left crankcase of the first Scout, which immediately went into a heavy schedule of test riding. The test results were even better than expected. A very rugged and, for its time, a very smooth-running V-twin engine produced more power than it should from its 37 ci (600 cc). The helical gear primary drive was a bit noisy but rendered a "solid" feel, particularly at slow engine speeds where there was no such thing as primary drive chain snap. Cautious decisions throughout development resulted in a little engine that was incapable of over-stressing the rugged primary drive and transmission. It wouldn't be long before the advertising guys would think up "You can't wear out an Indian Scout!" and they would be telling the truth. The compact double-loop frame was likewise very sturdy. Footboard vibration was far less than on the Powerplus twins with their old-style center-tube frames and tacked-on footboards.

The Reception

The Scout produced unbelievable power. Although the engine capacity was only 60 percent of the biggest 61-ci (1,000-cc) Indians and Harley-Davidsons, the output was closer to 70 percent of the big models. This, coupled with the lighter weight of the Scout, resulted in acceleration that was only slightly slower than that of the larger V-twins. The top speed of about 60 miles per hour compared poorly to the 75 to 80 miles per hour on tap from the big twins. But speeds above 60 miles per hour could seldom be sustained for more than a mile. It is far easier to ride 150 miles per hour now than it was to ride 60 miles per hour then. The roads of the era were simply too rough, with pavement usually ending at the city limits of middle-sized cities. Many streets were still unpaved, especially in smaller towns, while rural roads could be more accurately described as "trails." In fact, well into the 1920s there were maps that laid out national "motor trails." In other words, for a single rider, the Scout usually offered as much usable performance as any larger twin. Only in the case of hauling a passenger did the Scout fall behind, and only just so. The only preeminent quality of the big twins was their sidecar hauling ability.

The sporty performance of the Scout made the new model a double-barreled threat to all big twins, Indians as well as Harleys and Excelsiors. Simply put, the Scout was a model to please all riders, the motorcycle for "every man," to use the British term for such an elusive hoped-for motorcycle. Peppy output aside, the Scout was first and foremost a user-friendly motorcycle. The rugged Scout suffered none of the flimsiness of earlier lightweight models of Indian and its rivals. Yet alongside the 61-ci twins of Indian and rivals, the Scout looked much more a lightweight than a middleweight. The bike pleased men and women who swung a leg over the saddle and gave it the sit test. If they dared to learn to ride, they learned quickly, their confidence boosted by the low saddle position and the easy, almost hands-off handling that was not that different from a pedal bicycle. The low-slung layout counted big in this department.

Yet the Scout pleased the most rugged of riders in whose hands its lightness and agility more than compensated for its relatively small engine. Out in the real world, heading into deep ruts, a sandy wash, a muddy stretch, or freshly spread deep and soft gravel, the Scout came into its own when in capable hands. This motorcycle had it all.

Indian dealers immediately knew what they had. Telegrams and letters arrived at the factory by the dozens, raving about the new Scout. There were smiles all around and an attitude of "now we've got 'em," meaning Harley-Davidson and Excelsior couldn't hope to keep up. Sales were brisk. Indian's policy was to push the Scouts, because the new middleweight stirred up less sales resistance to pedestrians upgrading to the status of new motorcyclists. Besides, this year's Scout buyer could be next year's big twin buyer and why sell one new motorcycle when you could sell two? The publicity items displayed by Indian dealers, in the form of banners, posters, testimonial letters, and sales literature, almost gave the impression that Indian had only one model, the Scout. Typical of the approach was the "Indian Scout Club," a time payment scheme offered as if no other models were bought on time.

Going head to head against the Scout was the Harley-Davidson Sport, a 36-ci horizontally opposed twin (flat twin), laid out with the cylinders in line with the frame. The Harley Sport was introduced a year before the Scout, and was the first middleweight side-valve (flathead) model by a major American manufacturer. The Sport boasted a gear-driven primary drive and unit construction of the engine and transmission. Although the Milwaukee model was soundly engineered, it didn't catch on like the Scout. One old-timer offers an interesting theory: that the Sport didn't have the "correct" sound, the "potato, potato, potato" V-twin noise that had already captured the hearts of American enthusiasts. Apparently, the Harley-Davidson Sport also didn't have the power and speed of the Scout.

The success of the Scout immediately prompted the design of a new larger version of the model, which debuted late in 1921 for the 1922 season as the 61-ci Chief. The Chief was proudly termed "basically a big Scout." But even the introduction of an entirely new big twin Indian failed to overshadow the continuing importance of the Scout, as revealed by the factory to dealer publication "Contact Points" No. 8, November 15, 1921:

> The 1921 motorcycle and bicycle show is now history. . . . As usual, the Indian exhibit was second to none on the floor. In fact, the center of attraction at the entire show was the beautiful Indian Chief and Princess sidecar finished in gold and white with red upholstering. . . . But despite the approval of the new models, the fact remains that the Indian Scout held the center of the stage from the standpoint of Indian dealer interest.

1921 Scout Highlights

An additional luggage rack brace was placed on each side, so there were two braces on each side. The standard Scout seat was the Messinger Air Cushion. Electric lights and a generator were new options. The electrically equipped Scout had a generator takeoff drive mounted above the clutch housing. This required a different primary drive case and cover to interface with the bolted-on generator takeoff drive. The non-electrically equipped Scout may have used the same primary drive case and cover after earlier style cases and covers were phased out. The Scout rear stand had side members with a semicircular cross section like the Powerplus, instead of a channeled cross section.

1922 Scout Highlights

New for the 1922 Scout were the headlights, Klaxon horn, the Splitdorf DU-5 generator, the

Splitdorf S-2 magneto, a switchbox with built-in ammeter, and black finish of the handlebars (previously nickel plated). The primary drive cover, previously without writing, was labeled "Hendee Manufacturing Co. Springfield Mass. USA." The cover was fitted with an oil filler plug on the top, an oil drain plug on the bottom, and an oil level plug on the clutch cover face.

On the Scout cam gear case (timing case) cover, there was a new removable oil pump (earlier oil pumps had been cast integral with the cover). The rear wheel hub and brake drum were new. The front cam bushing in the cam gear (timing) case cover was new. The frame had a vertical seat post (or seat mast) in order to work with the new spring seat post arrangement; previously, this tube was curved. The kickstarter was mounted to the seat post—earlier kickstarters were mounted to the transmission case. The seat connection was wider and was mounted through the frame. In the transmission, new right and left countershaft bushings supported a new countershaft.

1922 All Models Finishing Services

The factory organ "Contact Points" No. 16, January 12, 1922, listed nickel-plating service available on any Indians per customer or dealer request. Parts that were routinely plated in nickel were: carburetor, cylinders, head plugs, handlebars, handlebar tops, and handlebar levers. The factory offered to repaint a number of parts, including front fork springs, luggage carriers, oil tanks, stands, sidecars, and fenders.

1923 Scout Highlights

For 1923, Indian changed the tanks to accommodate the side-mounted compression release rod. The new Corcoran-Victor headlight had a built-in switch. Optional horns were the long trumpet Klaxon or the Sparton (the latter per "Contact Points" No. 66, March 8, 1923). Indian replaced the aluminum switch box and built-in ammeter with a simple ammeter and separate switch as a cost-cutting measure. The carburetor manifold was new. The toolbox was moved from the luggage rack to the lower left side, and was connected to the battery box with a special bracket.

1923 Transcontinental Record!

Attaining superior results with a Scout required a rider with capable hands and sufficient nerve. Paul Remaly fit the bill. Riding a 37-ci Scout, Remaly broke the Canada-to-Mexico "Three Flag" record in May 1923, covering the 1,655 miles from Tiajuana, Mexico, to Blaine, British Columbia, in 46 hours and 58 minutes,

1924 Scout. In recent years, collectors have begun to favor original unrestored bikes, even when they're in this shape. Their philosophy: any motorcycle can be restored, but "original" status cannot be duplicated.

A new oil pump and round-section (rather than flat) gearshift lever were fitted to all 1924 Scouts. Longer and wider handlebars were a new feature. This early season example continues with the same "push action" front fork used since 1920.

breaking the record previously held by Wells Bennet on an 80-ci Henderson four-cylinder machine! A month later, Bennet barely lowered the record to 46 hours and 9 minutes. In July, Remaly then regained the Three Flag record on the Scout with an insulting time of 43 hours and 21 minutes. Remaly's average speed of 38 miles per hour was achieved over deeply rutted and boulder-strewn "roads" that would barely meet today's definition of the term. To place the achievement in context, think of it as a 1,655-mile trail ride. For that matter, one could buy a book of maps describing the nation's national system of motor "trails."

In August, his confidence boosted, Remaly set off on the Scout to attempt a new transcontinental record. Remaly used pilots in his epic journey because rural roads were seldom marked. Here's his recruitment letter to Indian dealers Smith and Enander of Rock Island, Illinois:

Portland, Ore
Aug. 18th, 1923

Smith & Enander,
Rock Island, Ill.

Dear Sirs:

I will leave Astoria, Ore., at 3 A.M. Sat. Aug. 25th on an Indian Scout in an attempt to lower the present Transcontinental Solo Record. According to my schedule I am due to arrive in Clinton, Iowa, at 2 A.M. Wed. Aug. 29th. I am wondering if you could have a man meet me in Clinton and pilot me across the state of Illinois.

Anything that you may be able to do in helping me put this record across will certainly be appreciated. You will be notified when I leave Marshallton, Iowa, and believe that you would do well to notify Bootz at Des Moines where to reach you so that there will be no slip up.

Thanking you in advance for any help that you may be able to give me, I am,

Very Truly Yours,
Paul Remaly

Holder Three Flag Record
[in hand-writing] P. S. I plan on sleeping awhile at Clinton.

With the preliminary arrangements nailed down, Remaly aimed his Scout into the darkness at 3 A.M. Saturday morning, and rode out of Astoria, Oregon. From here on, telegrams were exchanged between Remaly and various Indian dealers, to keep the support network informed. Here are samples:

CHICAGO ILL 1215P AUG 28 1923
C A SMITH LAFAYETTE HOTEL CLINTON
LEFT GRAND ISLAND FIVE ARRIVE CLINTON EIGHT
C G CRANDALL 1225P

DESMOINES IA 412P AUG 28 1923
C A SMITH LAFAYTTTE HOTEL CLINTON IA
REMALLY LEFT OMAHA ELEVEN FORTY FIVE LINQUIST WILL MEET HIM AT AMES AND TAKE HIM THRU SHOULD ARRIVE CLINTON ABOUT 6 PM
FREDERECK BOOTZ 440PM

EXTRA RUSH CHICAGO ILL 817A AUG 29 1923
CA SMITH LAFAYETTE HOTEL CLINTON IA
REMALY LEFT CEDAR RAPIDS EIGHT AM BE SURE AND MEET AND WIRE ME
C G CRANDALL 830A

Claude Smith guided Remaly across Illinois from Clinton eastward. Smith was an excellent choice, being an accomplished racer, hill climber, and motor drome (wall of death) rider. Smith recalled that, in addition to rain and heat, their biggest threat was the road, which was full of potholes and mud. Smith rode as fast and as hard as he could, never letting up in his all-out efforts. But any time he looked back, Remaly was only a foot or so behind. This amazed Smith, who had the benefit of a full night's sleep, whereas Remaly had been on the road for days and was surviving on catnaps. Success lay ahead.

R A CHICAGO ILL 1230P AUG 31 1923
SMITH AND ENANDER ONE FOURTEEN NORTH MADISON ST ROCKFORD ILL
PAUL REMALY ON INDIAN SCOUT ARRIVED NEW YORK ONE SIXTEEN AM STANDARD TIME

AUGUST THIRTY FIRST BREAKS TRANSCONTINENTAL RECORD BY TWENTY TWO HOURS THREE MINUTES
C G CRANDALL 237P

Remaly's time of 5 days, 17 hours and 10 minutes beat the 80-ci Henderson's time by over 22 hours! In their sales pitches, dealers Smith and Enander pumped up Remaly's record and their role in it. Today, Woody Carson, an active antique motorcycle enthusiast, recalls that he purchased a brand-new 1924 Scout from Smith and Enander because the little 37-ci bike was exactly like the one Paul Remaly had used to set a transcontinental record.

The Motorcycle and Allied Trades Association stopped sanctioning long distance road records in 1919, because they felt speed limit violations were bad publicity. Shortly afterwards, Indian announced that it would no longer support record runs over public roads, due to its position as a major supplier to police departments. But the point had been made; the Indian Scout offered as much "real world" performance as any motorcycle. Meanwhile, the rival middleweight Harley-Davidson Sport was quietly killed off at the end of 1923, a victim of Scout popularity.

1924 Scout Highlights

The 1924 Scout featured a new handlebar bracket (center part of the bars) that was split in one cut, from the left fork leg hole through the fork stem to the right fork leg hole. The idea was to clamp the bars to the front fork more securely in order to reduce vibration through the bars. The handlebars were longer and wider. In midseason, a new taillight setup had the license plate and guard brackets more securely welded, and the light riveted to the main bracket bent in an offset to absorb vibration. The gearshift lever was round in cross section, instead of a thin flat strip. On the clutch release foot levers on each model, a fold-up heel pad was provided. The new oil pump had a boss for the inlet angled 90 degrees to the body instead of angled down about 45 degrees. The rear stand had a C-channel cross section instead of a semicircular cross section. A new optional alloy piston was available.

Several changes were made midseason. A new pull-action front fork featured stronger tubing. A new front fender accommodated the new fork, with the connecting link (rod from the rocker arm to the springs) running outside the fender rather than through it. The inscription on the clutch housing was changed from "Hendee Manufacturing Co." to "Indian Motocycle Co." Larger wheel hubs were the same size as the Chief hubs. On the tanks, single-line pinstriping replaced the earlier double-line striping.

1925 Scout Highlights

The cylinder heads were removable, and the cooling fins pattern was changed from radial to fore-and-aft. The valve spring covers were new. The saddle suspension was changed from seatpost springing to conventional coil saddle springs, and the saddle height was lowered. A new combination of clutch plates was announced midseason.

1926 Scout Highlights

Optional "wire brush" (unpainted) "motor base" finish was available in 1926. Although the factory used the term "motor base," the wire brush finish also applied to the primary drive of the Scout and Chief, and to the transmission case and cover of the Scout, Chief, and Prince. Longer and wider handlebars were fitted with a new handbrake lever and a new horn switch. The switchbox with built-in ammeter returned, having previously been used only on the 1922 model. The new Schebler Model H carburetor had a different body casting.

In midseason, the new inlet manifold was threaded with large union nuts that drew the manifold up against the cylinder inlet nipples. (Earlier inlet manifolds were unthreaded and were retained by clamps.) Cylinder cooling fins were deeper and wrapped around the exhaust ports. As an accessory, the sidestand was first offered in May. The muffler was new. A new alloy piston was available.

1926: The Very First Scout Still in Service

Since the introduction of the Scout line for the 1920 season, Indian had proudly been proclaiming "You can't wear out an Indian Scout!" A measure of proof was offered in the June 1926 issue of *Indian News*:

> Right in Springfield, Massachusetts, there is being operated daily, at the office of the Indian Company, the very first Indian Scout produced. What's more, there is a sidecar attached to it. The machine was assembled in August 1919 and bears motor number 50R000. The speedometer shows a total mileage of 88,450 miles. The way it is standing up indicates that it will be in use for many years.

What Is "Product" Anyway?

The Scout and the newly introduced Chief were the better mousetraps that, according to folklore, would lead the world to Indian's doorstep.

They really were better motorcycles than Harleys and Excelsiors by most objective standards, being cleaner, smoother, quieter, and more rugged, and in the case of the Scout, being without a meaningful rival. But Indian was learning that there was more to the motorcycle business than building good motorcycles. The lessons Indian was learning are still true today. In the motorcycle field, on the most basic level, the product's purpose is rider satisfaction. This involves not only the qualities of a new motorcycle, but the attributes of the dealership, including dealer support in the form of readily available spare parts plus competent quick repairs.

Equally true then and now is the matter of image. Motorcyclists like either to ride fast or to feel that they can ride fast anytime they wish. The latter includes most of us, who are buttressed in our heroic self-image by the "halo" effect. In other words, if my brand wins the big races, then my bike must be a fast motorcycle and I must be a manly man (or trendy woman) to be riding it. There is always a market for "fast," and riders will endure much if they feel compensated by the speed image. The problem for Indian was that Harley-Davidson had won all the national championship motorcycle races of 1921! Among these impressive Harley victories was their fourth consecutive win of America's most prestigious race, the Dodge City 300. At this critical juncture, Harley-Davidson had become the go-fast bike in the minds of many riders.

Indian was learning that sound Harley-Davidson dealerships and the Harley speed image were keeping riders of the olive drab brand in the Harley fold. They were not riding over to the Indian shops to change brands. Brand loyalty ran deep in what amounted to a three-company industry. Following the brisk sales of the initial 1920 season, Indian business declined one-third in 1921, and in 1922 dropped to one-half of the 1921 level. This was the great turnaround period between Indian and Harley-Davidson. For the remainder of the 1920s, and extending all the way through 1938, Harley-Davidson outsold Indian two to one.

1925 Super-X Defines a New Concept

In late 1925 the Excelsior Motor Manufacturing & Supply Company of Chicago, builders of Excelsior V-twins and Henderson fours, scrapped their long-running 61-ci Excelsior. Replacing it was a sporting middleweight with a new name, Super-X. The Super-X would prove to be more than simply a new model, because it introduced a whole new category of motorcycle, the super sports middleweight. The new 45-ci F-head Super-X outdid the "something for nothing"

magic of the 37-ci Indian Scout. As well as having a displacement that was about 20 percent larger than the Scout 37, the Super-X 45 featured a very compact high compression cylinder head. Indeed, the specifications of the Super-X were such that oftentimes riders could not find fuel of sufficiently high octane to run the engines without detonation rearing its ugly head. This was particularly true on the West Coast, where some Super-X riders carried a small can of fuel additive to ensure knock-free performance.

By this time, there was hardly a dribble of competition for the three major companies: Indian, Harley-Davidson, and the Excelsior Motor Manufacturing Corporation. The tiny Reading-Standard company had stopped building big twins in 1922 and after six years of production (1920 through 1926 models) the Ace four cylinder was in its final throes with no visible market presence. The so-called "big three" were now quite close to being the sole mass producers of American motorcycles. In such a three-sided field, anything one company did was closely studied by the other two.

Before either Indian or Harley-Davidson built a 45-ci motorcycle, they went along with Excelsior/Henderson's desire for a new 45-ci competition class. In August 1926, on the Rockingham, New Hampshire, board track, the first 45-ci national championship race got underway. Surprisingly, the race was won on a 30.50-ci Indian single ridden by Jim Davis. But Indian was a near miss.

On paper, the Scout and the Scout-inspired Chief were world beaters. In the saddle, the Scout and its big brother delivered as advertised. But in the American motorcycle stew, there were many ingredients besides the quality of the motorcycles. The bikes were great, but Indian and its dealers were being outsmarted by a better-managed company, Harley-Davidson. The Scout couldn't overcome Harley-Davidson's speed image and brand loyalty. In the real world, there was a simple fact of life: the Scout and Chief had not transformed American motorcycling as they had been designed to do. In this most fundamental way, the "every man" Scout had both pleased and disappointed had done well, but not well enough.

This 1926 Scout rider's view is typical of 1920-1927 Scouts.

21

Chapter Two

The Happy Combination:

1927

As of 1926 there were two choices for Harley-Davidson and Indian: ignore the Super-X challenge or meet it head on. Here, the plot thickens, for Harley-Davidson had for some time already been planning a middleweight V-twin to compete with the Indian Scout. Although the middleweight Harleys arrived three years later, its subsequent problems arising from excessively light construction suggest that in 1926 the drafting table version had been laid out as another 37-ci model. At the January 1927 New York City motorcycle show, Indian debuted the Indian Scout "45" (conversationally, always "forty-five" and never "four-five").

The civilian version of the Scout 45 was, officially, the "Sport Solo." Said the sales literature: "What a motorcycle DOES show what it IS . . . Reaches top speed in a few seconds, throttles down to a walking pace with ease—carries you along miles and miles of highway with an instant flow of smooth, soundless energy . . . You'll have to try it—ride it, to really know how radiantly alive with pep and energy this new Indian really is."

The 1927 "Scout 45" had surprising power and acceleration, with Indian claiming the Scout 45 could accelerate from 5 to 65 miles per hour in 10 seconds. Police departments across the nation ordered many of the "Police Special" Scout 45 models, but to a great extent these police sales came at the expense of the larger Indian Chief previously favored.

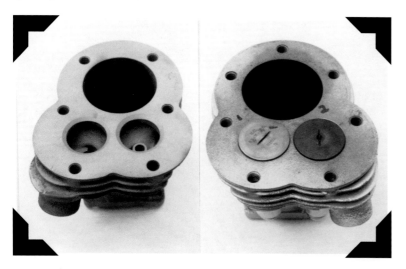

On the left is a rear cylinder from a 37-ci (600-cc) Scout; on the right is a front cylinder from a 45-ci (750-cc) Scout. The critical point: the bore of the larger cylinder extends right up to the edge of the inlet valve. The reason? To allow both the larger and smaller cylinders to work on the same crankcase. The happy accident? Better breathing and surprising power.

Thus, the presence of both the Super-X 45 and the Indian 45 Scout in early 1927 almost certainly motivated Harley-Davidson to go back to the drawing board and reengineer their "37" as another 45. Although none could know it, the ripples in this 45 pond would continue for the next three decades and beyond.

"Genius" is somewhat an overused word in the field of designing internal combustion engines. Progress typically comes in very small increments, and luck can be a factor. "Lady Luck" smiled on Indian, which more or less fell by accident into an unpredicted and fortunate outcome.

Trying to save dollars and time, Indian took a shortcut in engine development and gave up a design feature that was supposedly critical to air-cooled engine reliability. What they gave up was a cooling airspace between the cylinder bore and the valve "pocket," the chamber in which the valves were situated off to the side. This feature had long been thought to be essential in F-head and flathead engines. The process whereby the

The 1927 750-cc Scout 45 top speed of 70–75 miles per hour was about 20 miles per hour beyond that of the 600-cc Scout. The Indian side-valve (flathead) engine delivered real-world sporting performance via the simplest route. "Exotic" overhead-valve engines were in their developmental infancy; flatheads were the proven standard of the era.

Rider Bob Armstrong, a rising hillclimb and racing star, posed on a 1927 Scout 45. The rider's clothing and the bike's extra equipment highlighted items from the Indian accessories catalog. Armstrong's riding impressions were reported in the April–May 1927 *Indian News*. The Scout reached 65 miles per hour in 10 seconds, which was sporty for that era. *Baer family collection*

cooling airspace was given up was very simple. Engineers looked at the cylinders of the 37-ci Scout and wondered what would happen if they took the cheap way out, if they used the same castings as the basis for the cylinders of a new 45-ci engine. They determined that a bore of 2-7/8 inches was the maximum permissible, and when combined with a stroke of 3-1/2 inches, the outcome would be a volume of 45.44-ci. By "maximum permissible," the point is that the cylinder bore came within a few hundredths of an inch of intersecting the inlet valve seat. There was essentially no unused space between the bore and the inlet valve.

Back to the airspace thus forfeited. Certainly, on paper, the cooling airspace looked like a sure winner. But on paper, there is a tendency to view things ideally, one of these envisioned ideals being a smooth laminar flow of air moving parallel to the cooling fins. Smooth airflow is ideal to heat transfer. But once again, the "real world" had a lesson to teach. Either directly by experiment, or more likely by happy observation and consequent

analysis, Indian learned that in the real world the flow of air over the cooling fins was anything but smooth. Disturbances that caused buffeting air included: the angle of the cooling fins in relation to the horizontal, the front wheel and fender, the frame, the forward-mounted magneto, the fuel/oil tank, and the rider's legs.

Indian may have also figured out, or may have simply happily accepted, a point later understood in the course of engineering the Indian Four of the early 1930s. When it comes to cooling, the issue of metal versus air is not a simple one. The existence of a "cooling" air-space between the cylinder and the valve pocket came at the expense of the "heat sink" attribute. In other words, without the air pocket the generated heat had a large volume of metal in which to dissipate, and the front of this heat sink was directly in the air stream. Whether understood fully or simply accepted, the result was that the "quick and dirty" solution did not have the theoretical drawback of excessive heat buildup.

So what? Here's what. The key to the impressive performance of the Indian 45 Scout was this close proximity of the cylinder bore to the valves. The popular phrase is that the engine breathed well. The unquestionable proof of the point came over a decade later, when Harley-Davidson arrived at the same conclusion in its racing versions of the Harley "45" (they never gave this model a name). (Harley's late 1930s solution was to angle the valves inward from the bottom near the tappets, so that the valve heads were close to the cylinder bore.)

In the words of Indian record setter Roland "Rollie" (rhymes with holy) Free, the Indian Scout 45 was "just a happy combination of stuff that seemed to work." Happy indeed. Before the Indian versus Harley street wars ended about two decades later, hot stuff "breathed-on" Indian 45 motorcycles, those that benefited from careful assembly and tuning, would outrun 61-, 74-, and 80-ci big twins of both brands.

A Road Test

Writing for *Indian News*, former Wigwam staffer Ted Hodgdon reported on his road test of the new Scout 45. The period piece was full of exaggeration and imagery, as were most motorcycle articles of the era. But the promotional article gives us an insight into the motorcycle expectations of the day, and of the sales pitches that would be made by Indian dealers to prospects. Hodgdon always wrote in the irritating "royal" plural mode, so brace yourself.

Smoothness

. . . We rode out of the yard, and the very first thing we noticed about this new Indian was its smoothness. It purred along as smoothly as a six-cylinder car. If it was not for the deep-toned, purring exhaust, one would not think there was a motor there—unless he accidentally twisted the throttle too suddenly—and then the realization would come that there is either a motor or dynamite under him. There seems to be no vibration point at any speeds, and mechanical noises from the motor are conspicuous by their absence.

The next thing noticeable about the Scout 45 was the acceleration. And when we say acceleration we mean just that! The motor answered instantly to the slightest touch of the throttle, and showed signs of having all kinds of pep—but, just to see for ourselves how much pep it had, we slowed her down, slipped into second gear, and then opened the throttle suddenly. The Scout 45 acted just like a wild animal! Perhaps the front wheel didn't come up in the air, but it certainly felt light when those extra

From the sales literature: "Note the deep cooling fins on the head and in the area of the exhaust ports to ensure ample cooling under all conditions . . . Now notice the generous size of the intake manifold—and its length, which means speed plus economy. This highly efficient design, found throughout the Scout 45 powerplant, accounts for its phenomenal performance."

From the sales literature: "Why the Indian Scout 45 is a Police Special: Has the acceleration required to get the jump on the fastest cars . . . Low weight distribution, keen balance . . . Low saddle position and smooth vibrationless power output reduce riding effort and fatigue . . . Left hand throttle leaves gun hand free . . . Economical, reliable, and comfortable. . ."

horses in that powerful 45 motor came to life. There was a roar and a leap, and then it was hard to breathe [author: Come on! Give us a break!], so we ducked our head [author: Should it be "heads" rather than "head"?] and shifted into high. As the clutch went in again there was another leap and then we were too scared to do anything but shut her down. You see—in just the time it takes to say 10

According to oral history, Indian built 26 45-ci overhead-valve motorcycles in 1926. Although built in 1926, the overheads were first raced in 1927 in order to promote the new 45-ci Scouts with side-valve (flathead) engines. Most of the engines were fitted to hillclimb bikes, but some were mounted in bikes raced on board tracks and flat tracks.

words, the Scout 45 motor had snapped us up to 60 miles per hour, and it surprised us. Don't wonder [why] they call it the Police Special—any Motorcycle Cop anywhere can catch a car with that acceleration. The Scout 45 surely packs a powerful wallop in both barrels. It's a real he-man's motorcycle.

Speed—A Lot of It

The next thing was a speed test, so we turned off the Boston Post Road onto a road which looked fairly smooth. With feet well back on the boards, both knees gripping the tank, and head well down (a la Curly Fredericks) we opened up the throttle gradually. Right away things began to take on a different aspect. The landscape changed into a blur—and the whole day changed into a screaming, rushing wind, which beat and tore against this lowly scribe—as if trying to blow him clear off into space.

Enough, already, of 1927 prose. We have a feel, now, for the corn. But the larger point is that the Scout 45 was indeed a fast motorcycle for the era. Hodgdon went on to cite a top speed of 74 miles per hour according to the speedometer's maximum-speed hand, and this over what he termed a short stretch of road, implying more

speed was on hand. "Yes sir! 74 miles per hour. . . ." The remaining headlines in the article were: "A Great Hill Climber" and "Easy Handling." Hodgdon concluded with, "Gee! Where have you been all my life?"

1927 Scout Highlights

The new 45-ci Scout motor included the major changes required for the new capacity. New flywheels increased the stroke from 3-1/16 inches to 3-1/2 inches. The 45-ci bore was 2-7/8 inches, up from the 37-ci bore of 2-3/4 inches, so this meant new cylinders and cylinder heads.

Other changes applied to both 37- and 45-ci Scouts. New larger camshafts reduced noise, improved valve timing, and prolonged life. In the transmission main shaft, an end plug in the shaft diverted oil circulation to the clutch plates. For late-1927 Scouts, optional cast-iron pistons were offered for riders who preferred a quieter running motor. The front fender had a valance (side coverage). Alemite grease fittings were installed. The compression release pull-rod mechanism passed "through" the tank via an open-ended built-in tube (instead of alongside the tank and through a bracket). On the tank sides, beneath the large

"Indian" script was the word "SCOUT" in small all-capital block letters.

A lower riding position was achieved with the new saddle. The "semi-bucket" saddle had a crescent-shaped metal stamping to support the rider's buttocks, but the center and forward parts of the saddle consisted solely of leather stretched over a frame of heavy "wire." The saddle thus conformed to each rider's anatomy. Beneath the saddle, a small metal fitting was attached to the forward part (pommel or nose) of the leather. This fitting rode on the wire subframe, so that by screw adjustment the leather top could be either relaxed or stretched tighter.

An electric-motor-driven ("oogah") horn was available as an accessory on all models. The foot brake lever was larger and relocated. A new battery box was mounted lower and had a removable side. Scout mufflers had a new tailpiece. Early-season models had a shorter exhaust system; late-season models had a longer exhaust system. A new under-seat forging secured the new wider rear frame structure (rear fork). The rear fender was longer, had two braces (instead of one) on each side, had drop sides, and a removable brace.

The Overhead-Valve Scouts

The documentation is long gone, but the oral history passed through longtime Indian enthusiast Sam Pierce many years ago asserts that 26 45-ci overhead jobs were assembled in 1926. These 45-ci specials were built for the newly established 45-ci class for racing and hillclimbing.

Special features of the 45 overheads included two camshafts running in self-aligning ball bearings, and a ball-bearing crankshaft. The big ends of the connecting rods ran on roller bearings, while the little ends used a plain (journal) bearing. Two oil pumps were mounted to the timing case cover. The rear pump supplied the crankshaft and connecting rod big ends, while the front pump supplied oil to the lower rear of the front cylinder. This was to compensate for the lower amount of oil slung to the front cylinder by the crankshaft, rods, and flywheels. The earliest 45 overheads had iron cylinder heads but later examples were fitted with aluminum heads. The engines ran on alcohol and sported a 15:1 compression ratio.

Beginning in 1927, the overhead-valve 45s were used in all three of the major competition venues, board track racing, dirt track racing, and hillclimbing. Hill climbing equaled racing in prestige. Both Orie Steele in the east and Swede Matson in the west won major hillclimbs. Not

The two camshafts ran in self-aligning ball bearings and the crankshaft was also ball-bearing mounted. The first few engines featured cast-iron cylinder heads but later engines such as this one featured aluminum heads. On some engines, a second oil pump was fitted to the bare circular boss on the bronze timing cover. In the two-pumplayout, the front pump lubricated the rear wall of the front cylinder, because the front cylinder received less oil splash from the flywheels, crankpin, and connecting rods.

content with honest Scout successes like Paul Remaly's record, the Indian company threw around the Scout name after these hillclimb victories achieved on 45-ci overhead-valve specials. Although the connection was tenuous, the theme of these mid-1920s ads was that the lucky buyer of a standard Indian Scout was, somehow, going to experience the same performance as the professional riders of the special racers.

The Happy Combination

Meanwhile, the regular 45-ci flathead Scout was strong enough to convert many riders for whom previously only a 74-ci model had been sufficient. The 45-ci Scout "Police Special" met the standards of many police departments. A top speed approaching 80 miles per hour was more than could be safely used on most of the roads of the era, satisfying sport riders as well as cops. The Scout 45 was indeed the "happy combination."

Chapter Three

Greatest of All Indians? Series 101 Scout:

1928–1931

Indian had been lucky. Their 1927 Scout 45 was a happy combination of ingredients stumbled upon in a quick cost-saving approach to fielding a sporting middleweight. While the speedy Scout 45 was impressing hundreds of dealers and thousands of riders, the Wigwam fell into another pot of gold, with the engineering department moving easily toward a substantially improved midseason model. But early in the 1928 season, it appeared another year of minor refinements.

This shot mimicks period advertisements. "'Some smooth ride!'—you'll say . . . Never have you experienced such sidecar comfort as this 'sweetheart' model now offers. A real comfort for the Indian Scout (Series 101)—the machine that motorcycle fans are going crazy about." (Indian magazine advertisement)

An unknown rider poses with a 1928 Series 101 Scout in front of the main entrance to the Indian factory. This may be the very first Series 101 Scout, a prototype, which is suggested by the muffler clamp on the lower rear frame tube. On all production Series 101 Scouts, the muffler is hung from an extension dropping down from the sidecar-mount forging near the rear axle. No such extension is on this motorcycle. *George Yarocki collection via Butch Baer*

The traditionally shaped Scout, beefed up with the 45-ci engine, was treated to customary detail improvements.

Early-1928 Scout (short frame) Highlights

Front brakes were provided for the first time, as a midseason change. A Chief-size front hub was mounted in a strengthened front fork frame, which was required for the front brake. The motor was mounted with a through-bolt setup, which had a long bolt passing through the extended front part of the crankcases. The angle of the frame front-down tubes was changed, to work with the new motor-mount setup. The bottom of each front-down tube entered a forged elbow that also joined the lower frame tube on that side.

Indian replaced the black headlight rim with a nickel-plated version. The instrument panel was mounted to the front fork and just behind the handlebars (instead of to the frame above the tank) and included a new ammeter. The ammeter was operated by induction action provided by two loops of wiring behind the case. A button now operated the horn, and new handle grips were provided. New, longer footboards had rounded front and rear edges. The new generator was a Splitdorf DU-7. The electric-motor-driven horn became a standard feature, and the horn was moved to the left side, beneath the tank.

The new timing case cover accommodated the new oil pump with a horizontal plunger. An oil shutoff line was added. The taillight featured a new "solid" (not braided and not flexi or helical) cable casing.

Company press releases labeled the new saddle, still of semi-bucket design, "Chief size." It was suspended on 13-coil saddle springs instead of 10-coil springs. The footboards were mounted with a greater incline, as on earlier Chiefs. Brake and clutch foot levers were farther forward. The clutch lever was mounted from the left front down tube instead of from a plate attached to the primary drive. Exhaust pipes were attached to the cylinders with nuts instead of the cone-style mounting previously used.

The new battery box was mounted lower on the left lower frame tube. The top of the battery box was about 3 inches below the top of the toolbox, instead of on the same level. The Scout now featured the same air intake cap introduced a year earlier on the Chief.

A new tailpiece appeared on the muffler. For the first time the Scout used the same rear brake as the Chief. The new brake featured an external contracting band instead of an internal expanding band, and was moved to the left side of the wheel. Archival photos indicate this brake had earlier appeared on 1927 export models, so this may have been a mid-1927 change on domestic models. The Scout required a new transmission case to accommodate the new ball-bearing drive gear.

1928 Series 101 Scout Highlights

In the March 1928 motorcycle magazines announced the new Series 101 Scout. Parts books of the era list the first 101 Scout parts as 1929 parts, so some argue that the 101 Scout was in effect an early-release 1929 model. The principal differences from the pre-101 Scout were the longer wheelbase, powerplant moved forward, lower saddle, a more graceful upper frame tube, and a more graceful fuel-oil tank. The 101 wheelbase was 57-1/8 inches, compared to 54-1/2 inches for the earlier models. Saddle height on the 101 was 26-1/4 inches, compared to 28 inches for the earlier models.

The Series 101 featured a bullet headlight. An inverted "Y"-shaped bracket suspended from the center of the fork held the front fender. The handlebars had a new shape to match up with the lower seating position. The new Mesinger saddle (still semi-bucket) could be adjusted to three different positions relative to the saddle springs, in order to suit varying rider weights. No photos prove the availability of contrasting color tank

panels, but this styling feature may have been initiated at some point during the 1928 season.

Indian moved the powerplant forward about 3 inches, which had the effect of making steering more positive. The longer 101 wheelbase permitted the battery to be placed directly behind the powerplant. The 101 toolbox was new and was mounted about where the earlier models had carried the battery box. The combination of fork rake and trail, low center of gravity, forward powerplant positioning, lower saddle height, and increased wheelbase gave the 101 Scout unique handling qualities. The 101 Scouts seemed (and still seem) to boast both stability and agility, which are normally opposed qualities. They became the favorites of trick riders and remain popular with them even today.

No Annual Models

From 1928 through 1930, Indian had an official policy of "no new annual models." The company emphasized that improvements would be incorporated into factory production as soon as practical rather than waiting until the following model season. The term "Series" was used to emphasize that the new 101 Scout was neither a late-1928 model nor an early-1929 model. Meanwhile, it has become customary within collector circles to refer to the 3-1/2 years of 101 Scout production by traditional model years, since there are identifying characteristics that separate one machine from another on what amounts to annual changes regardless of the factory's disavowal of this process. This has left a small debate among some 101 enthusiasts as to whether the initial 101 Scouts released mid-year in 1928 are more properly termed late-1928 or early-1929 models.

45 Overhead "Scouts" Dominate

In 1928 the new 45 overheads supplanted Charlie Franklin's amazing 61-inch flathead Powerplus-based racers as the fastest in the Indian tribe. As the late Jim Davis remembers it, their speeds approached 140 miles per hour during practice runs over a five-mile circular course at Muroc Dry Lake in Southern California. This sounds too high to me, but Muroc is a windy place. (I know; I lived there at Edwards Air Force Base in the 1970s.) Speeds this high over part of the course indicated strong tailwinds and excessively tall (lower ratio, numerically) gearing, which would produce slower lap times than desired. If true, the tall gearing suggests this session was more about the riders having fun than seriously practicing.

The lightweight compact Sweetheart sidecar was in response to the popularity of the Series 101 Scout. The rider is George Yarocki and the passenger is his wife, Milli Yarocki. The sidecar striping has since been changed to a darker Napier green.

1928 Indian Wins All!

The year 1928 saw Indian return to its racing supremacy of decades past. The iron redskins won all of the national championship races. Included were dirt and board track records in the 45-ci class. Jim Davis' 25-mile 45-ci board track record was achieved with an average speed of 115.37 miles per hour.

1929 Series 101 Scout Highlights

Indian produced the unofficial 1929 models from July 1929 through March or April 1930. On July 15, drop-center rims replaced clincher rims, and straight-side 4.00x18 tires replaced 3.85x18 clincher tires. New "Timken" taper roller-bearing wheel hubs were fitted. Contrasting color tank panels were offered. The through-the-tank compression release pull rod was replaced by a simple toggle on the timing case cover. From June 1929, all carburetor bodies were die metal instead of cast. On the rear brake rod, which connected the cross shaft and brake, a clevis was added to the front end.

Indian Beats 61s with 45s!

The 45-ci racing class was so popular that in April 1929, Indian announced it would no longer support anything but the 45-ci class in hillclimbs.

Riding factory-designed 45 overheads, Orie Steele and Howard Mitzel placed first and second in the 61-ci class at a big hill climb meet in Enfield, Massachusetts. Jim Davis won the only 45-ci national championship of the year. Californian P. A. Bigsby designed, and his employer, Los Angeles Indian dealer Al Crocker, built a number of kits for converting flathead Scouts into overhead Scouts. These Crocker-built overhead-valve Scout conversions appeared nearly identical to the factory design, although some experts can readily distinguish between them.

1930 Series 101 Scout Highlights

The unofficial 1930 models were probably produced from March or April 1930 to March or April 1931. Indian introduced chromium trim in accord with a worldwide trend. A larger Moto-lamp headlight had a chromium-plated embossed rim; Indian claimed a 300 percent improvement in lighting. On November 25, the company announced that frame numbers had been initiated—earlier Indians had motor numbers only. (Indian charts don't show the frame numbers until 1931—this was an oversight.) The taillight wiring was protected by a flexible (spiral wound) metal casing and the taillight wire and casing were given a half-loop near the rear fender

hinge. A hinge on the rear fender assisted in wheel removal and installation.

Monkey Business at the Expense of Motorcycle Business

Indian fell behind in the sales war with Harley-Davidson, partly because of differences in how the two companies were owned and the ways in which they were operated. Since the departure of cofounders George Hendee and Oscar Hedstrom in the 1910s, New York banking interests owned and controlled Indian. This situation had come about because Indian had raised its initial operating funds by selling stock, and had likewise grown the company through a number of issues of new stock. Conversely, Harley-Davidson founders borrowed money to start the company, and their demonstrated knack for profit had enabled them to borrow all additional funds required to grow the company.

The contrast in management control between Springfield and Milwaukee is revealed by the startling difference in the operation of the board of directors of each firm. Since the law required at least an annual meeting of the board of directors, Indian had such a meeting. The annual Indian board meeting lasted an hour or perhaps less, with the minutes of the meetings published on a single page, amounting to little more than, "Hey, we had a meeting." These annual Indian board meetings were held in New York City, as the key men in the control network didn't want to be bothered with traveling to Springfield. It also seems they didn't want to learn anything about the motorcycle business. Practically speaking, Indian was under the control of absentee landlords.

At Harley-Davidson, the board of directors met monthly, and on occasion more often. The minutes of their meetings survive, and reveal that the three Davidson brothers and Bill Harley were calling all the shots: engineering, production, sales, and the necessary financing of the entire enterprise.

From an April 1941 internal Indian report comes the following retrospective summary of the shenanigans of the Indian Motocycle Company:

> During 1929 and 1930, the company engaged itself in the manufacture and distribution of lines not directly related to the principal products. These so-called unrelated lines included outboard motors, shock absorbers, electric refrigerators, ventilators and automobiles, and the engaging in the manufacture and sales of these lines resulted in a decrease in the working capital position of the company of approximately

1928 Series 101 Scout. "You've never known a ride like this! The flight of a bird, the grit of a bull dog. Power, get-there comfort and freedom! Over the hill and far beyond—go places, see things. Health, happiness, education! . . . Alone when you want to be alone—the Scout makes its own trail—or take the family in a sidecar. No better friends than those, who like yourself, know and heed the call of the open-road." *Indian sales literature*

The 1928 Muroc Races

as recalled by Jim Davis

It didn't make any difference to me what I rode [Indian or Harley-Davidson], 'cause I figured one was as good as the other. I picked out where I wanted to go, picked out the better events.

We were racing in Rockingham with our 45 overheads. At Rockingham, they were running around 120-122 miles an hour. We shipped from Rockingham, New Hampshire, to Los Angeles. The factory shipped the equipment out there, and I was supposed to go out and ride it. They weren't supposed to open up the equipment until I got there, and I didn't get in there until Saturday morning. One reason why the factory didn't want them opened was that they [dealers and riders] said the equipment they [the factory] sent out never would run. Crocker wanted to know if I was going to practice, and I said, "No, I don't need no practice because I ride 'em all the time." So they took 'em [the motorcycles] up to the lake.

Petrali was there [Muroc], I know. Somebody said Petrali was doing 140 miles an hour [in practice], and I said, "That, I want to see!" Just prior to the race, we had an old Travelair and we flew up. On our way up, we didn't have enough horsepower to get over the mountains, so we followed the pass up through. When we came into the lakes [dry lakes], we came right over the concession stand, and we're gonna loaf in, without any horsepower, see. And the bottom fell out of it! Hell, we fell about 100 feet! [chuckle] And the struts went out, broke both tires on this plane [chuckle].

My coup and stuff is at the airport, at Western and Beverly, that's about where it was then. And my riding clothes are in it. Everything I've got is in my coupe, locked up. And here it is Saturday, and the race is Sunday. But the equipment [motorcycles, etc.] is going to be up there. So when I rode [raced] up there, I borrowed a pair of overalls, coveralls, off a guy, and a helmet off another guy, and a pair of goggles off somebody else, and I had black and white sport shoes on. And Al Crocker, he was crazy; he said, "The factory sent you out here and this is the way you do?" "Well," I said, "it's an emergency."

I had the two [motorcycles] there, and I knew Freddie [Ludlow] would like to ride. So I asked him, "You wanta ride, Fred?" And he said, "Yeah, I'd like to." I said, "Well, there's two machines. Take your pick. Either one of 'em." And he said, "Well, you've been riding one, mostly. What's the number of the one you rode?" I told him. He said, "Well, I'll take the other one."

But we got the race underway. Dad gum, he [Ludlow] broke a valve spring on the one he ran, and of course mine didn't. Mine ran all the way through the program. I won the 25-mile national and the 5-mile open, and I think I got second in the 50. I should have won it without any trouble, but I just got a little bit too smart. I lost the pace and they ran away from me (chuckle). We averaged, I think, a little better than 113 miles an hour in that 25-mile national, which is what I went out for. And, as I say, I was fortunate and won the thing. I think in a trap out there, I ran 154 miles an hour, just with the wind in one stretch. [Author's note: this must be a memory problem for Jim.]

Jim Davis on the Indian overhead-valve 45 at Muroc Dry Lake, California. Renamed Rogers Dry Lake, the large flat expanse is at Edwards Air Force Base and is now the backup landing strip for the space shuttle. *Jeff Pearson collection*

After the race, see it was on government property and you couldn't charge admission. A lot of times the motorcycle clubs had these buckets with a little lid fastened on, and a little slot in it. That night at the motorcycle club in Los Angeles, we were opening up these tills, see, and in there was buttons, slugs, chewing gum, everything [chuckle]. I don't think they got much money. Like on the entry, if it was 10 miles, anybody that rode in it had to pay 10 dollars. This was something unusual. And in the 25-mile event, we still only had to pay 10 dollars. There was probably 10 or 12 riders in the program.

So it [the club] ended up [with] a little bit [of money], and they paid just first and second money.

I know I got, in my batch of stuff that I had, I had one of Joe Petrali's expense checks, which was 125 or 130 dollars—I don't remember which. That was in my pay envelope [chuckle]. And I opened it up, and I was looking at it, and I called Joe and said, "Look what I got here." "Yeah,"he said, "that's the way I had to enter." I gave it back to him. We used to have some nice programs up there [Muroc]. We never made much money but we had a lot of fun.

Incidentally, Davis beat Ludlow by 2 feet in the 25-mile feature. It was Ludlow's last race, as he decided to retire after over a decade of professional racing.

Up-and-coming hillclimb star Frenchie Castonguay posed on a factory hillclimb bike in a courtyard of the Indian factory in this circa 1930 photo. A conventional side-valve Scout engine was mated with a Powerplus primary drive and in a Powerplus racing frame. The entire running gear was the same type as that of the Gene Rhyne overhead-valve hillclimber. *Baer family collection*

$1,250,000. In the closing months of 1929, the production of unrelated lines was discontinued.

"What's all this?" you ask. It was all about the manipulations of a management group without a long-term commitment to building and selling motorcycles. The interest of the group, headed by president Louis Bauer and later by president Charles Levine, was strictly in the short term. These projects were introduced with much bally-hoo, and by tying in the famous "Indian" name with new products, the management sought to bid up the value of their stock holdings with a view to selling out and leaving new investors holding the bag. This practice, termed "pumping up" the stock, could have earned them a jail term.

Finally, the joy ride of the short-term group ended. Francis du Pont and his brother E. Paul took over Indian in the spring of 1930, ousting the Levine group.

An Eyewitness

We turn now to the recollections of Allen Carter, longtime employee of the du Pont family.

I went to work for DuPont [DuPont Motors] as an apprentice boy when we were building auto-mobiles, in 1925. About 337 DuPont automobiles were made—it was 335 or 337. At the time they were very expensive. They sold for about six thou-sand dollars. That was a lot of money back then.

The 1930 Series 101 Scout featured a new and larger headlight. "The man who rides Indian knows no boundaries . . . his world is measured by the length of the broad highways. His are the out-of-the-way places on the side road . . . Do far horizons beckon? Kick the motor over . . . give it the gas."

Mr. du Pont and his brother Francis I. du Pont had quite a bit of stock in Indian Motocycle. Indian was having a problem—this was during the depression—and this guy Levine had control of things. Mr. du Pont got wind that he was selling machinery out of the plant. He was stripping the place to help the finances.

So Mr. du Pont and his brother Francis went in and bought enough stock that they took control. He was protecting what he already had, by buying enough stock to control the company, and got rid of Levine. He actually didn't buy the company. What he did was to take over the controlling interest of the thing.

I was close to Indian, because Joe Hosley was our manager at DuPont Motors. When Mr. du Pont took over Indian, he took everybody from DuPont Motors [including Hosley] to Springfield, and left me in Wilmington for service [of DuPont automobiles].

President du Pont, Technically Involved

As a boy, E. Paul du Pont assembled a kit motorcycle, a feat that required machine shop skills. At Du Pont Motors, he personally designed the first engine used by the cars that bore his name. When he took over Indian, du Pont's natural technical interests were focused on the motorcycles and he enjoyed returning to the sport of motorcycling. His correspondence with Indian General Manager Loren "Joe" Hosley contains numerous discussions of motorcycle technicalities. From a November 30, 1930, letter to dealer Harvey Erickson of Minneapolis:

. . . Concerning the dry-sump lubrication, we already have two machines on the road making experiments with this, and your thought of an extra oil supply is very valuable to us. This will receive careful consideration. One gallon is a good deal of oil to carry, however considerable weight would of necessity be carried high up on the machine. It is also difficult to get this much extra bulk high up on the machine, and at the same time maintain a low center of gravity and seating position . . . . I am much interested in your stating that the tank on the Scout is the right thing, as our Sales Department report that the two tanks concealing the frame in the Chief, and the Harley-Davidsons, are the only thing, and that we must have this to be in the running. Personally, I don't like the idea because the Scout type of tank is, from an engineering standpoint, far superior to the split tank and never gives trouble, whereas the split tank springs leaks.

Paul du Pont's Unofficial Test Riders

Allen Carter continues:

Of course, Mr. du Pont was always interested in motorcycles. That's why he bought into Indian, because he was a motorcyclist.

When Mr. du Pont took over Indian he sent down one of every model that they were building. We ran those, Mr. du Pont and I, and Charles Moran, who was a test engineer for DuPont Motors. We would ride them all the time and make suggestions. Mr. du Pont rode the motorcycles himself, too. We found a lot of things. They never had a decent headlight because the generator never

Circa 1930: The Worcester, Massachusetts, "Armstrong Roamers" club plays a match of motorcycle polo, with Scouts in abundance. *Armstrong family collection*

Newly bought by a German Jew in 1933, this 1930 Series 101 Scout was soon abandoned and left in a cellar. In 1989, Scottish enthusiast Alan Forbes smuggled the bike a few pieces at a time through Checkpoint Charlie at the Berlin wall. "Why so many passport stamps?" a curious guard once asked. "To visit my girlfriend," Forbes replied. A week later, the wall came down. (The original magneto was off for repairs when this photo was taken.) The Scout stands outside Cramond Tower on the estuary of the river Forth, close to Edinburgh, Scotland. Built in the 14th century and originally occupied by the Bishops of Dunkeld. *Robbie Smith*

charged enough to keep the battery up, you know. But anyway, we did a lot of work. We didn't actually work on the motorcycles; all we did was found out things and told Mr. du Pont, and he went back up to Springfield and tried to get Joe Hosley to do it. That was during the Depression, and they had no money up there to do anything. They were just hacking along. In fact, I was surprised that they ever brought the Sport Scout out. I don't know where they ever got money enough to do that.

An example of the unofficial test rider group effort is contained in a letter of March 31, 1931, from E. Paul du Pont to Loren (Joe) Hosley, Mr. du Pont's General Manager at Indian:

The second thing I notice is that there is in the Scout that I have received a frightful noise in the generator drive. From actual tests we find we can hear this five-eighths of a mile away. We discovered that the generator drive belt guard was acting like a sound box, and on removing this guard the noise was reduced so that it could be heard only one-eighth of a mile away. As you will realize, sound decreases with the square of the distance, this is some reduction in the sound. I am told that the noise disappears in about 4,000 miles. I would suggest that you take a few machines at random and observe this noise on the street, or in the yard [internal factory courtyard] if you do not wish to get them dirty. The noise is not actually increased by engaging the clutch in gears, so that a good account of it can be obtained by idling the motor.

1931 Series 101 Scout Highlights

Instead of the traditional enamel, Indian used DuCo lacquer for the basic finish. Spokes were cadmium plated instead of painted black. A new Indian-face horn was mounted below the headlight. A running change to mid-1930 models became officially introduced on the 1931 models; this was the chromium-plated embossed headlight rim. The headlight was center-mounted instead of side-mounted. The handlebars were reinforced by a crossbar.

On the tanks were new transfers, with smaller Indian script and the model name placed beneath the script. For the first time, the generator was an Auto-Lite unit, the data plate number being GAS-4102. The rear wheel was detachable, and was secured by three long stud bolts and three driving pins. The accessory speedometer was axle driven instead of cogged-wheel driven.

The new oil pump was throttle controlled and had a different appearance. The muffler was new and the cutout was reinstated. Indian wanted to eliminate the cutout due to unfavorable publicity,

but rider demand forced the return of this feature. The rear brake drum was moved to the right side.

Aluminum pistons became standard equipment and cast-iron pistons became optional. On cast-iron Scout pistons, a new crosshead (wrist, or gudgeon) pin was retained by a lock ring instead of a dowel pin.

The Hot Stuff "B" Motors

Information contained in "Contact Points" No. 429, June 5, 1931, enabled dealers to convert regular Scouts to "B" motor specifications, effectively stopping the factory monopoly on "B" motors. These features, however, had been in use for some time. Most of the "B" parts weren't listed for Scouts in subsequent parts books, though they may still have been available as special order items. The "B" motor parts included: front and rear cylinders, intake nipples, cylinder heads, inlet and exhaust valve springs (the same as on Chiefs), Schebler DLX-81 carburetor (the same as on Chiefs), carburetor manifold (Chief size), manifold cone, and manifold union nut.

A Personal Guarantee

Mr. du Pont, a resident of Wilmington, Delaware, was perturbed that the county police department apparently was considering changing from Indians to Harley-Davidsons. This was unthinkable to E. Paul du Pont, who penned the following letter dated March 31, 1931:

Mr. Alban P. Shaw, County Engineer,
New Castle County, Wilmington, Delaware.

My Dear Sir:

This is to advise you that the Indian Motocycle Company will hearby guarantee, and the writer personally endorses this, that motorcycles sold to the County under the pending bids are guaranteed as to material and workmanship, beyond the 90-day period up to and

41

Twenty Days Without A Stop!

A team of riders, passengers, and pit crews shared round-the-clock nonstop duties that propelled this outfit to a new endurance record of 20 days! The Scout endurance run beat the best airplane endurance run by 57 hours and 3 minutes, and the best automobile endurance run by 77 hours and 21 minutes. *George Yarocki collection via Charles Moore*

W. E. "Si" Dietz, Indian dealer for Bangor, Pennsylvania, organized an impressive record outing for a 1929 Series 101 Scout. A team of six riders rode a Scout sidecar outfit around and around the Nazareth County Fair Ground half-mile track, nonstop, for 20 days! They started on September 28, each man riding for an hour and resting for five hours. Trackside, a fuel man kept track of the mileage and signaled when refueling was required. The motorcycle and sidecar were then slowed down to 10 miles per hour, so that the refueling man could run alongside and step into the sidecar with his gas can. The crew made over 200 refuelings, over 100 oil fillings, and over 500 rider changes at the 10 miles-an-hour pace. Fuel consumption averaged about 49 miles per gallon, and oil consumption averaged about 110 miles per quart. The fuel mileage was typical, but at 10 miles per hour the oil consumption was extreme, the team obviously having chosen over-oiling as a form of insurance.

At one point in the marathon, pounding rain forced the team into half-hour shifts for three days. At other times, riders felt good enough to ride several hours at a turn. The 101 Scout lapped the track over 25,000 times, accumulating 12,695 miles before water finally made its way inside the magneto and the ignition failed. After removing the magneto cover, the inside was wiped down and the motor restarted within a few minutes, but the endurance run was over.

The American Motorcycle Association (AMA) officially sanctioned the run and made secret checks at irregular intervals to see that the team didn't cheat. Except during the 70 hours of driving rain, high (third) gear was used throughout the run. During the rainstorm, the rig ran in second gear for 48 continuous hours, which was probably some sort of unofficial record. Although "You can't wear out an Indian Scout," was the Wigwam's slogan, it was certainly possible to stretch the rear chain, as the team proved. According to the Indian News account, every three or four days the riders slowed down and took up the slack in the chain. One is left to wonder just how they did this while on the move, but perhaps at a steady 10 miles per hour in high gear there wasn't enough torque and acceleration at the rear axle to misalign things during wrench turning. The Scout endurance run beat the best airplane endurance run by 57 hours and 3 minutes, and the best automobile endurance run by 77 hours and 21 minutes.

including what should be the reasonable life of a motorcycle.

This guarantee is made in consideration of your accepting the order of Indian Motocycle Company of which I am President.

Yours very truly,

E. Paul du Pont

In show biz terms, the 1927 Scout 45 was a hard act to follow. But in the 101 Scout, Indian had another winner. Yet, there was that one big problem: because it was costly to manufacture, the 101 Scout wasn't the moneymaker Indian needed.

The 101 Scout had become something of a cult bike among Indian dealers and the hardcore, hard-riding fans of the Indian marque. The Indian 101 Scout was just a better bike than the rival Harley-Davidson 45. This conclusion was obvious to anyone without strong brand loyalty, though there were few such riders at that time.

It must have therefore been a troublesome matter for E. Paul du Pont to conclude that the popular 101 Scout was to be discontinued for the 1932 season. This decision began to take shape in

the first year of Mr. du Pont's presidency, as seen in the following extract of a December 3, 1930 letter from General Manager Loren "Joe" Hosley to E. Paul du Pont:

I have talked to Mr. Franklin about sending you the blueprint of the gasoline tank, but I find that he has held up on all of this due to the redesigning of the frame to fit both the Scout and the Chief. There is still another deal in that he is working on a new fork similar to the English style, which would again alter the gasoline tank but would make a much better condition in that the tank could be moved further forward and would not have to clear the fork.

The letter reveals the plan to produce the Scout in a modified version of the Chief frame, thus the "Scout" in lieu of the "Series 101 Scout." Also of interest is the discussion of a girder fork, either of the style later used on the small twin dubbed the "Scout Pony" or of the style later used on the Sport Scout.

Thus, E. Paul du Pont and his Indian Motocycle Company were dealing with the paradox of the Series 101 Scout, at one and the same time both successful and disappointing. More on this later.

43

1931 Series 101 Scout. "The new handlebars give more restful riding position and better control. The new headlamp mounting allows better aiming of the light, and a new high frequency vibrator horn with a special Indian design face is placed beneath the headlamp. The new tank panel makes for a more handsome combination of colors." (Indian sales pamphlet). Another important 1931 feature was a throttle-controlled oil pump, so that oil delivery depended on the throttle opening as well as engine revolutions.

The 101 Scout in Retrospect

Decades later, as the men who had ridden 101 Scouts entered their middle age, they looked back fondly on the model as an all-time great. Writing for the February 1946 *Motorcyclist*, C. Trumbell Jr. termed the 101 Scout:

. . . one of the most practical and well-known two-wheel thoroughbreds . . . No other motorcycle was ever adapted to so many purposes. Some of the forms it took were: sports machine, hill-climber, racer, commercial delivery van, sidecar record breaker, army mount, and police job. Strange as it may seem, it performed all these duties well. As a solo sports machine, it gave the rider over 75 miles per hour, and with a little work such as installing a larger manifold and carburetor, high cams, planed heads, etc., an honest 85 could be squeezed out. Many of the "hot shots" soon learned that by using flywheels with longer throws, a red-hot 57-cubic-inch stroker could be had. These mongrels could leave most big twins on acceleration and top speed.

One such machine, built up and ridden by "Red" House of Washington, D.C., was electrically

Made from the original factory archives negative, this picture depicts the 1931 Series 101 Scout. Note the new oil pump with a horizontal cylinder. Its adjustment was the opposite of preceding pumps, and must have caused a few mistakes along the way. At the pump bottom, a cable communicates the throttle setting so that output can vary according to throttle opening as well as engine revolutions.

timed at 104 miles per hour in a two-way run, and I daresay others have done as well or better. As a hill-hopper the 101 had no equals in its class, and the very violent takeoffs used in this sport proved that the gear drive primary unit and the transmission could really take it.

As a racer, the 101 was seen on every track in the country, and plenty of firsts were copped by riders of [101] Scouts. The late Jessie James rode to fame on this model which he used for years after the new 101s were no longer coming out of the Wigwam. Jessie also held the Class C speed record of 101 miles per hour with his Armstrong Scout [author's note: named for dealer/sponsor Erle "Red" Armstrong] . . .

As a police machine, the 101 was perfect, although they were not quite fast enough for real highway patrol. For city work, however, many a poor cop would be happier today with a light Scout instead of the 600-pound heaps they're using now. The Army got a lot of service from them too . . . From the foregoing, it is easy to see that a dealer selling 101s was sitting pretty. No matter what the customer wanted to use the Scout for, the Scout was made to order; if the 101 wouldn't do what the buyer wanted, one could assume that he didn't want a motorcycle in the first place.

The last of this line, 1931, was as trouble-free as any machine known to me. As far as servicing them goes, it was a mechanic's dream, for the whole machine could be overhauled with a minimum of effort and special tools. The average workman could have the complete motor and transmission out of the frame and on his bench in the time it takes to remove the gas tanks on most modern jobs. If a man couldn't overhaul the complete machine, motor, transmission and all, and have the job all road tested in an eight hour day, he'd better quit and get a WPA [author: President Roosevelt's Works Progress Administration] job learning on a shovel.

There were other less verbose but powerful endorsements of the 101 Scout. Legendary Harley-Davidson racing tuner/designer Tom Sifton offers his opinion of why Harley-Davidson brought out their 1928 high performance 74 (note: 74!) -ci "Two Cam" twin:

101 Scouts cut such a swath, and Harley didn't have anything ready, so they put the two-cammer in a road frame, in '28.'

[Author's note: Sifton built the racing motorcycles of stars Sam Arena, Larry Headrick, and Joe Leonard.]

Circa 1931: Cordy Milne on a Scout-powered "short track" (today, "speedway") racer. These races were run over 1/4-mile-or-shorter cinder-surfaced tracks. The frame appears to be a cut-down Series 101 item. Milne had a great speedway career, finishing third to brother Jack's first in the 1937 World Championship. (American Wilbur Lamoreaux was second, all riding J.A.P.-powered bikes, not Indians). *Baer family collection*

Santa Monica, California, Indian dealer Charles Moist named his fishing yacht "101." Moist had for years pitted for Sport Scout star Ed Kretz, yet his soft spot was for the 101. One of the four cofounders of The Antique Motorcycle Club of America, Emmett Moore, conducted his own 50-year road test of his 101 Scout. Sport Scout record setter Roland "Rollie" Free relates:

That [the 101 Scout] was, in my opinion, the best motorcycle that Indian ever built. The gear primary was a little whiny, but nothing ever happened to them—nothing. The actual design of the frame and everything, I preferred the 101 (over the Sport Scout). The Sport Scout had bigger cylinders, better manifolding, and all that stuff, more cooling. The Sport Scout was an easy motorcycle to make run, very easy, [but] you could've done the same thing in the 101 frame.

Some of the Series 101 Scout's charming qualities would still please riders, if presented in a modern equivalent: low-down geometry, more-than-adequate power, lightweight, simple construction, rider maintainable, ruggedness that minimized repairs, and, not the least, that hard-to-achieve feeling of both agility and stability. The 101 Scout was an affirmation of an old saying among architects: "More is less." There wasn't a lot to the 101 Scout— no extra stuff hanging on it—but what was there was good. For its time, what was there was fabulous.

Chapter Four

Cutbacks, Make-do, and The Soul of Indian:
1932–1939

The economic depression had deepened since it began in 1929. Motorcycle production for the calendar year 1931 was 4,557, which represented only about 15 percent of factory capacity. Moreover, the steady decline appeared likely to continue indefinitely. The survival of the Indian Motocycle Company was now at stake. The inklings of E. Paul du Pont's decision to scrap the 101 Scout were provided earlier in the December 3, 1930, letter from Hosley to du Pont.

The 1934 45-ci Sport Scout replaced the 1933 stop-gap Motoplane. Of similar "keystone" frame layout to the earlier bike, the Sport Scout featured more robust construction and the important improvement of an integrated powerplant similar in function to that of the Chief and the old Series 101 Scout. The powerplant concept was achieved by bolt-up of the engine, primary drive, transmission (gearbox), and associated mounting plates to form a single unit.

The 1932 Scout replaced the popular Series 101 Scout. The new Scout featured the 45-ci engine in the same frame used for the 74-ci Chief. The new cylinders with larger inlet and exhaust ports had previously been offered only on the hot stuff "B" motor Series 101 Scouts. Riders demanded the new style of "saddle" tanks with the top frame tube concealed. On the downside, twin saddle tanks were always more prone to leakage than the earlier single tank fitted between the top two frame tubes.

chosen victim? With the absence of any dialog on the matter in the dribble of surviving company records, one can only speculate.

Here's my speculation. First, the cost issue: The 45-ci 101 Scout (and the few 37-ci 101 Scouts) cost as much to manufacture as the 74-ci Chief. This is because the cost of manufacturing a motorcycle is a function of the number of parts in the bike, and the smaller components in the smaller models have a negligible cost savings impact. For this reason, customers expected a bigger priced differential than Indian could provide, tempting the company to bid up the selling price of the Chief in order to bid down the selling price of the 101 Scout. But the big twin Chief was a hard sell against the Harley-Davidson 74. To some extent, this was because Harley-Davidson had long emphasized the big twin field while Indian had diffused its sales strategy by having two big bikes, the 74-ci Chief and the 78-ci Four.

The constant Scout emphasis in Indian's advertising had reaped the reward of good Scout sales, but profit margins weren't adequate. Scout sales, in effect, had come at the expense of Chief sales. Both the Chief and the Four offered a better chance to make sales at an acceptable profit. The Four had somewhat of a captive audience among the many police departments favoring it for smoothness and ease of starting, and customers were prepared to pay a premium markup to get its

Finding difficulty in meeting the monthly payroll, drastic measures were in order, and one drastic measure was eliminating the Series 101 Scout. Granted that Indian needed to reduce the number of models offered, why was the 101 Scout the

This 1932 Scout Pony is either unrestored or is a decades-old restoration. Indian built the 30.50-ci flathead Vee-twins to appeal to first-time motorcyclists. It was America's lowest price twin-cylinder model, retailing initially for $225, or about one-third less than the popular 74-ci Chief. The price of the little twins would eventually fall to only $195.

Factory competition rider-turned-model Woodsie Castonguay posed on a 1932 Scout Pony. The only accessory on the bike was a speedometer. From a sales pamphlet: "The new Scout Pony is light in weight, easy to handle, economical to run—yet is every inch a he-man's motorcycle." *Baer family collection*

luxury features. Thus, from an economic point of view, the 101 Scout was the most vulnerable of the tribe. Yes, Indian had the better middleweight model, but Harley-Davidson was "crying" all the way to the bank because most riders—Scout publicity notwithstanding—preferred big twins. Mr. du Pont thus made a sound business decision by killing the 101 Scout. This substantially reduced factory operating costs and paved the way for a less costly line of new small motorcycles to compete on the low end of the market.

The styling issue: Although the 101 Scout was an outstanding performer, its styling was considered a bit old-fashioned by most riders. Indian's big twin Chief, and all Harley-Davidson models featured a "saddle" tank layout in which the top frame tube was hidden by the fuel "tank" (actually, a pair of tanks drawn up together to appear as one unit). Considered graceful by today's collectors, there's no denying that the 101 Scout styling was less appreciated in 1931 (see du Pont letter of November 20, 1930). Of course, a saddle tank layout could have been adapted to the 101 Scout, but it seems Mr. du Pont was thinking ahead to a more contemporary middleweight motorcycle as popularized in Britain and Europe. The Indian 45-ci engine could later be housed in a more stylish package, once money wasn't so scarce.

The New "Scout"

As alluded to in the du Pont-to-Hosley letter of November 20, 1930, the new "Scout" was in fact a 45-ci engine installed in the Chief frame. The 101 Scout riders greeted the new Scout with a hoot. Heavier and less responsive was their verdict. Much maligned by writers, including myself in previous books, I am now second-guessing myself and others, as a result of riding a 1935 "Scout." The example I rode was a charming cosmetically unrestored 1935 bike belonging to Bob's Indian Sales of Etters, Pennsylvania. I found the bike quite peppy and as rev-happy as any Sport Scout. I felt none of the expected heaviness, although surely a one-after-the-other comparison test with a 101 Scout would have favored the 101. It seems, then, that much of the opposition to the 1932 Scout was emotional. At a suggested retail price of $295, the Scout was but $30 cheaper than the battery-ignition Chief at $325. But that was a nearly 20 percent difference. The new Scout was also priced 5 percent under the 1931 45-ci Series 101 Scout ($310), and just 4 percent above the 1931 37-ci Series 101 Scout ($285).

Once again, as in the case of the 101 Scout, there couldn't have been much profit for the Wigwam. Some police departments favored the Scout over the Chief, buying into the argument

This young lady, Florence Burnham, showed off her new 1932 Scout Pony. Extra-charge items included custom striping on the edges of the front fender braces, front safety guard, speedometer, white shifter knob, lambskin saddle cover, chrome-plated exhaust system, luggage rack, and saddlebags. Note that the tank striping and script differs from the Castonguay bike. *Baer family collection*

that the smaller model would prove less costly to operate. This seems unlikely to me, in that a slower turning and less stressed engine is likely to also be more reliable. Still, the Scout I rode had its own charm, and a case could be made for the 1932 Scout simply on the score of how it felt to ride one. The weight difference of 35 pounds felt much bigger. (The 1932 Scout ride reminded me of my days in the 1960s as a salesman of new Triumph motorcycles, when the 500 cc models felt so much more agile than the 650-cc models.)

1932 Scout Highlights

The radically different appearance of the 1932 Scout is evident from the illustrations. Not only was the Scout engine placed in the Chief frame, but the Chief frame was also completely new in order to achieve the style proven popular in transatlantic motorcycling. In vogue were a taller steering head and teardrop "saddle" tanks that concealed the upper frame tubes. Because of the greater length of the upper frame tubes, front down tubes, and fork, these were heavier in order to sustain required strength. The new "solid" steering head, front hub, and leaf-spring assembly were also heavier. Consequently, the weight of the new Scout was 427 pounds while the weight of the earlier Series 101 Scout was 399 pounds.

The front-wheel hub, fork frame, and fork leaf spring were wider. The Scout/Chief frame was equipped with a new Timken roller bearing for the lower steering head section. The frame had a "nicked out" (smaller and flat) area on the lower

left rear tube near the tire, to mount a siren on police models. On non-police models, this flat area could be seen under the rear portion of the toolbox. On the right tank, a "cofferdam" (space) was placed between the fuel and oil sections, which made impossible the mixing of fuel and oil due to leaking solder. Optional lighter compression and tension saddle springs were offered. Also, the rear saddle support bracket had four adjustments for different rides.

For the first time since 1911, magneto ignition was optional instead of standard. The new standard battery ignition system operated on the wasted spark principle. Both cylinder plugs fired on every motor revolution, with one plug firing normally, near the end of the compression cycle, and the other firing near the end of the exhaust cycle. This system dispensed with the need for a distributor, but required extra battery power. Although the cost of the magneto was saved, the cost savings weren't minimized because the contact breaker unit was driven by the same series of gears as the magneto. Harley-Davidson had used the wasted spark principle for many years. Both cast-iron and optional aluminum pistons featured new piston pin (gudgeon pin) lock rings made from wire that was 0.015 inch heavier.

1932 Finish Details

The unpopular Duco lacquer finish was replaced by Dupont DuLux enamel. (Some exuberant riders of 1931 models had polished completely through the thin lacquer!) Late 1932 Scouts may have had black cylinders instead of nickel-plated cylinders; the parts books aren't clear on this. Customers could order special plating of individual items. No special package was offered, but a year later the more frequently requested items were grouped together at a single price. The more frequently requested special plating included cadmium rims and the following chrome items: handlebar, including clip, screw, and cover plate; carburetor air horn; bumper retainer and screw; valve spring covers; taillight body; and exhaust tubes. Although the listed items were the more frequently requested, customers also ordered special plating on other items. Incidentally, special plating was already an old custom, as detailed by many reports of stolen machines in "Contact Points" in the 1920s.

A Bike Especially for the Depression

To field a model more in keeping with the stark economic situation, Indian offered a "new" small V-twin of 30.50-ci (500-cc) capacity for the 1932 season. How was the Wigwam able to design

and build a new motorcycle at this dreary time? By making the "new" model largely the offspring of an earlier Indian. Christened the "Scout Pony," the little twin was essentially a twin-cylinder version of the 21-ci (350-cc) single-cylinder Prince of the late 1920s. Major commonalities included the fork, fenders, primary drive and housing, clutch, and transmission. Engine components were doubtless interchangeable, and the Scout Pony frame was hardly more than a modified Prince frame. The styling was updated with the now-obligatory saddle tank arrangement.

The Scout Pony was announced midseason, in the June-July issue of *Indian News*, and was offered at the suggested retail price of $225. Translation is in order for Depression-era prices, which are otherwise a foreign language. The little twin was priced 24 percent under the $295 Scout.

"Pony Will Exceed 70 Per," headlined the *Indian News* road test. Road tester Reggie Pink bragged about the Scout Pony's handling through sharp curves and over dirt roads.

A sharp right turn and the dirt road became a sand "highway" with an average depth of 6 inches. Back to second—throttle wide open—and the way she glided through—was a picture to watch. Under absolute control every second of the time. Indian's racing department had exerted their influence,

penned Pink. The entire front fork itself is similar in action to the ones used in the fast Indian 45 hill climb machines ridden so successfully by Orie Steele, Howard Mitzel, and Gene Rhyne. The new clutch and gear box also embody the lessons learned through competition. Large man-sized exhaust pipes carry the heat away from the cylinders to a neat, efficient silencer. The throttle controlled oil pump feeds directly to the big-end bearing, thus assuring an adequate supply of lubrication under all conditions. Yes, it looks as though the racing department has supplied a lot of data for this job, and I dare say we are going to see Ponys pulling off a fair share of the competition of the future . . .

1933-A New 45-ci Twin

The 1933 models included the new 45-ci Motoplane, which was identical to the Scout Pony except in engine capacity. Apart from the word "Motoplane" in small letters beneath the Indian script on the tank sides, the only way to tell the difference in the two models was to count the cylinder cooling fins; there were six on the Motoplane and five on the Scout Pony.

All the 1933 twins featured circulating dry-sump oiling. There were problems with over oiling and under oiling, and the dry-sump system would not settle down until the 1935 season. Still, even at

A rare jewel, this original unrestored 1932 Scout (or Standard Scout) has the "new" feel of a low-mileage machine. The bike even has original distributor stickers.

By using the Chief frame, production was simpler and less expensive than with a dedicated Scout-only frame. Lacking the low and compact feel of the Series 101, the new model met with rejection from many sporting riders. Nevertheless, these are charming bikes that are much more nimble than the companion Chief big twin. In the background are the "Olgas" mountains of the Australian outback.

A cost-cutting feature of the 1932 Scout was the elimination of magneto ignition. A circuit breaker unit, driven by the same train of three gears used on previous magneto-ignition engines, resided in the space normally occupied by the magneto. The "wasted spark" system, without a distributor, fired the plugs on both the compression and exhaust strokes. The magneto-gear-driven unit was a one-year-only feature.

its worst state of development, the circulating lubrication was an improvement over the old "total loss" gee-I-hope-so lubrication. There was no more hand pump and no more guessing about whether to add or not to add a shot of oil.

The year 1933 marked the lowest ebb of the Great Depression. The Wigwam's production dropped to 1,667 motorcycles, which was about 5 percent of the factory's original single-shift capacity! Hardly any 1933 Indians are on the scene today. The Motoplane was destined to be a one-year-only model. I'm aware of only two surviving Motoplanes, and neither of these passed my way during the production of this book.

From *Indian News* for November-December 1932:

"Mere words can hardly describe the Motoplane—you've got to ride it-crack open the throttle-experience a new thrill of acceleration-this new Indian will obey your every whim instantly!" Weighing 349 pounds compared to the 1931 101 Scout at 399 pounds, the Motoplane must have indeed been quick on the getaway. The Motoplane fared even better against the 427-pound Scout.

Perhaps it was too quick. According to motorcycle historian Harry Sucher, problems were

experienced with the combination of the powerful 45-ci motor and the lightweight Scout Pony frame, which had a tendency to whip under acceleration. Restorer Robin Markey of Bob's Indian Sales (Etters, Pennsylvania) believes the transmission also wore excessively in Motoplanes.

1933 Scout Highlights

Dry-sump (circulating) lubrication replaced total-loss (non-circulating) lubrication. There were spinoff changes. There was no auxiliary hand pump in the right tank and no related oil line to the left crankcase, but there was an oil return line from the pump to the tank oil compartment. Changes to the right crankcase accommodated the new dry-sump oil pump.

The standard battery ignition system was changed. The magneto-style drive gear train was eliminated by mounting the circuit breaker on the timing case cover and driving the unit from the rear camshaft. There were several spinoff changes to the right crankcase and timing case cover. On battery ignition Scouts, the bushings for the former gear train drive were eliminated. Bosses were added to the timing case cover to mount the ignition system components, and to simplify production these bosses were also on the timing case cover of the magneto-ignition Scouts. In order to drive the circuit breaker, the rear camshaft was

longer on the outboard end and was keyed to mate with the breaker.

The headlight had a different rim and an adjustable lens. The convex headlight lens had a square pattern in the middle, and had the word "MOTOLAMP" in raised letters on the lens exterior. Cylinders and cylinder heads were black (this may have been a mid-1932 change). A chromium-plating option was listed, which included the handlebar (including clip, screw, and cover plate), carburetor air horn, bumper retainer and screw, valve spring covers, taillight body, exhaust tubes, cadmium rims, and sundry other parts. Altogether the package contained a total of 17 or more separate chrome-plated items. The fork was changed to accommodate the new scissor-brake anchorage.

1934 Color Explosion!

In 1934, Indian offered a total of 24 standard no-extra-cost one-color and two-color paint schemes. Moreover, special colors (white and silver cited as examples) were available for a $6 surcharge, and special striping and special panels were offered for a surcharge of $2.50 each. This year was the high point in terms of the number of no-extra-cost paint schemes, which had been growing since 1930. The special colors option remained company practice throughout the 1930s and 1940s (except war years 1943–1945), though

On this 1934 Sport Scout, the small circular cap fitted to the timing cover and beneath the rear cylinder is the circuit breaker for the "wasted spark" ignition system fitted to 1933, 1934, and 1935 battery ignition Scouts, Sport Scouts, and Chiefs. The one-piece rear chain guard is a 1934-only item. The "dog-bone" fork damper adjusters are incorrect; black disk adjusters should be installed. The motorcycle stands beside Borthwick Castle in the Scottish Borders. *Robbie Smith*

Indian documentation hasn't surfaced for some of these years.

1934 Scout Highlights

Indian changed the primary drive of the 1934 Scout from gears to a chain, and the chain case and cover had different shapes from the earlier primary drive case and cover. "Indian" script was added to the cover. The left crankcase main shaft flange differed in its interface with the primary drive case. Both the right and left crankcases lacked transmission case mounting studs because the transmission case was bolted to the engine. Indian introduced a new T-slot alloy piston. The cast-iron piston didn't change. The new alloy piston used a new oil control ring.

1934-The Sport Scout!

The Sport Scout was announced to dealers in the January 1934 issue of *Contact Points*, the factory-to-dealer publication. The Sport Scout caught some of the same criticisms as had the "Scout" (with the Chief frame) from fans of the Series 101 Scout. To a certain extent, the complaint was that the new model simply wasn't the beloved old 101. (Harley-Davidson went through the same reactions when their 1930 big twin flatheads replaced the 1929 F-heads.)

But the Sport Scout design was not in keeping with Indian's long tradition of cradle-framed motorcycles, a tradition begun with the original 1920 Scout. In design philosophy, the new Sport Scout owed more to the 1932–1934 Scout Ponys than to the 1920–1928 Scouts and 1928–1931 101 Scouts. Up front, the fork was a girder unit, the same in principle as that of the Scout Pony and Motoplane. A set of aft mounting plates held the engine and transmission together and attached to the rear frame section, and a set of forward mounting plates secured the front of this powerplant package to the front down tube. The front frame section consisted of the steering head, the single front down tube, the upper angled tube and the lower horizontal tube connecting the steering head to the vertical seat mast, and the vertical seat mast itself. The bottom of the rear section bolted to the transmission mounting plate, and the top of the rear section bolted to the forging at the top of the seat mast.

The new layout gave the Sport Scout a very light look. The absence of any frame structure beneath the powerplant contributed to this light appearance, as did the dull plated front and rear mounting plates. The weight quoted in the sales literature (probably without fuel) was 385 pounds, as compared to a claimed weight of 399 pounds

for the 1931 Series 101 Scouts and 427 pounds for the 1934 Scout.

Uncertainties

Why this frame design was chosen is unclear. Certainly, it would have been easier to store the small front and rear frame sections and to move them about the factory than was the case with the

old Series 101 cradle frames. But this seems hardly more than a minor convenience. The 15 pounds of weight-saving seem inconsequential. A manufacturing disadvantage was the fact that the powerplant had to be assembled with the mounting plates, and the front and rear frame sections then had to be bolted together. The mounting plates themselves had to be drilled out on a fixture to ensure proper alignment. These several steps replaced the earlier and simple-as-can-be cradle frame into which the 101 and earlier Scout powerplants had been easily dropped. All of this spelled more time, hence more manufacturing cost. It seems likely to me that the 45-ci Sport Scout actually was a more expensive motorcycle to manufacture than was the 74-ci Chief! As to the fact that a number of bolts and

"Girls Take To Motorcycling Too," said the ad in a 1939 magazine. "Because expenses are low; it's easy to get through traffic; it takes one out in the open air . . ." In the foreground, the young lady is mounted on a 1939 Junior Scout.

fork offers more resistance to small road irregularities than does the leaf-spring fork. This is because almost all of the girder fork weight is unsprung, while almost all the leaf-spring fork weight is either fully sprung or partially sprung.

These factors bring to mind the thought process and the scheduling that culminated in the introduction of the first Sport Scouts in mid-1934. Recalling the words of Du Pont employee Allen Carter: "I was surprised that they ever brought the Sport Scout out. I don't know where they ever got money enough to do that." Considering that a new form of stock (unmodified) motorcycle racing, Class C, was established for the 1933 season, could Mr. du Pont and other factory managers already have had this in mind when embarking on the Sport Scout design? Strange indeed, how a factory operating at about 5 percent of its capacity, and at the lowest point in the Great Depression (with no assurance things would improve), could find money to proceed on a new design during the year 1933. Although we will never know the whole story, know what was cunning and what was blind luck, we might just as well credit E. Paul du Pont and his staff with the foresight to produce a topnotch motorcycle for American racing.

New "Y" Motors

The high performance Model 634-Y Sport Scout was announced in January 1934. The "Y" motor was probably made available later in 1934 on the Scout (with Chief frame). The main feature of the "Y" motors was the "Y"-shaped inlet manifold and the correspondingly reoriented inlet ports on the cylinders. Thus the term "Y" motor.

The 1934 parts book doesn't include either the Sport Scout or the "Y" motors, but the 1934 "Y" motor configuration I assume to be the same as described for 1935 models. "Y" motors used the new so-called "trench" heads. The trench heads featured a sort of V-roof like a house. Commonly thought to be low compression heads due to the additional cylinder head height above the piston, the trench heads actually had the same compression ratio as the earlier heads, about 5.4:1 in the case of the Chief. These figures were obtained by measurement.

Keeping the same compression ratio was achieved by tucking in the head volume around the lower edges where the head mated with the cylinder, and by gradually letting the combustion chamber roof climb to its peak. The resulting configuration was sometimes termed a heart-shaped combustion chamber. The combustion chamber might be more accurately described as a Mickey

nuts were tightened to achieve frame rigidity, this would seem discomforting. How often did they have to be re-tightened?

In my opinion, the built-up Sport Scout layout presented only one clear advantage. The layout maximized ground clearance by doing away with horizontal frame tubes on either side of the crankcase. This was important only when racing, when the absence of these lower frame tubes around the powerplant would permit the Sport Scout to be banked over at a greater lean angle than would be the case with a cradle frame. Another departure from 101 Scout practice was the Sport Scout wheelbase, which measured 56-1/2 inches compared to 57-1/8 inches for the 101. This produced greater agility but less stability, making the Sport Scout wheelbase better for racing though perhaps not as good for road riding. The shorter wheelbase in the 1934–1940 Sport Scouts (with unsprung rear wheel) provided a much more choppy ride than given by the 101 Scouts.

The changeover from a leaf-spring fork to a girder fork seems as much motivated by style as by function. On the one hand, the girder does offer more travel, thus yielding a softer ride across really big bumps or holes. On the other hand, the girder

Circa 1936: Kenny Scholfield and his customized Series 101 Scout. Scholfield rode his motorcycle 90 miles to the 1936 southern California Muroc (Dry Lake) Speed Trials. He was clocked at 107.14 miles per hour on this motorcycle, which he then rode home. His was the fastest non-hauled bike of the meet. All runs were timed in one direction only and were wind assisted— but 107 miles per hour on a Series 101 is still amazing! *Scholfield collection*

Mouse shape when viewed from above, with the ears representing the valve areas and the face representing the piston area.

1935 Scout and Sport Scout Highlights

For 1935, Indian fitted new alloy pistons with reinforced head in the Scout and Sport Scout. Connecting rods were fitted with 12 long rollers instead of 24 short rollers. The right crankcase incorporated new camshaft bushings and new pushrod guides to work with new pushrods. New four-piece "clam shell" valve covers (four for each valve) mated with the larger pushrod guides. Cylinders had thicker valve guides, and cast-iron cylinder heads had a new shallower combustion chamber (see illustration). New "tulip" inlet and exhaust valves had thicker cross sections immediately below the valve head, but were interchangeable with earlier valves. New high-lift cam profiles were standard equipment. Both inlet and exhaust valves used heavier springs.

On Scout motor numbers BCD-334 through BCD-544, the front cam assembly oil pump worm drive on the camshaft was changed from a single thread to quadruple threads; Sport Scout incorporation point is unknown. With the quadruple-thread drive, a new smaller (from 7/16 inch to 3/8

1934 Sport Scout. The front of the crankcase main shaft boss has a 1934-only shape because it facilitates a 1934-only generator drive belt (rather than a drive chain). Magneto ignition wasn't offered, hence there is no magneto takeoff drive accommodation in the two o'clock position of the clutch cover. Also, the primary cover is narrower because the 1934-only system used a two-row chain (instead of a three-row chain). Black cylinders were used in 1934.

This 1935 (Standard) Scout incorporates the new fenders and Indian head tank decor popularized by the 1934 Sport Scout. In the background, Darling Harbor of Sydney, Australia.

inch) oil pump plunger was fitted, and the oil pump body was changed to accommodate the smaller plunger. On Scout motor numbers BCD-545 and later, the front cam assembly oil pump worm drive on the camshaft was changed from quadruple threads to double threads; Sport Scout incorporation point is unknown. Although retaining the same diameter, the oil pump plunger for BCD-545 and later differed in that it mated with the new double-thread drive. The 1935 cylinders and iron cylinder heads were nickel plated instead of painted black. Although optional angled aluminum cylinder head fins were first pictured in the 1936 parts book, these may have been a mid-1935 change. If so, 1935 optional aluminum Scout/Sport Scout heads were made in two cooling fin styles: with fore-and-aft fins and with angled fins.

The Scout was fitted with the same style of streamlined front and rear fenders introduced on the 1934 Sport Scout. However, the Scout front fender had a deeper valance (as did the Chief and Four). Both the Scout and Sport Scout were offered with an optional "V" or "Arrow" tank panel or with the plain tank panel available since 1928 or 1929.

1935 Highlights Unique to the Sport Scout

Numerous design changes on the 1935 Sport Scout indicated the 1934 model had been rushed into production. The more important of the changes simplified servicing. A drawback of the 1934 generator belt drive was that changing a belt required removal of the clutch and the entire primary drive mechanism. So the generator drive was changed from belt to chain. The new arrangement required reshaping the primary drive case and the left crankcase.

On the 1934 Sport Scout, the primary drive case was secured directly to a lug near the bottom left of the vertical seat mast. It was impossible to remove the entire powerplant as an assembly engine, primary drive, and transmission. This was prevented by interference between the shift-lever and shift-detent bosses of the transmission case with the lower left frame lug on the seat mast. Therefore, on the 1935 Sport Scout the upper rear "motor" lug was narrowed, and a spacer was interposed between the primary drive case and the seat mast. This permitted the complete powerplant assembly to be lifted up and off the front frame section.

Of necessity, the Sport Scout chain guard was deeply dished at the juncture with the upper-right-rear

frame tube. Consequently, the 1934 one-piece rear chain guard could be removed only after removing the rear fender and rear wheel. But the rear chain guard had to be removed in order to change transmission sprockets or work on the kickstarter mechanism. Therefore, the 1935 chain guard was made in two pieces joined near the vertical support tube on the rear frame assembly.

Other changes were made to strengthen the Sport Scout. The built-in 1934-only Sport Scout kickstarter wore excessively. So the 1935 and later Sport Scouts had a separate iron starter mount bolted to the rear of the transmission case. The fork shaft diameters were enlarged. The fork crown and stem assembly ("T" fitting at the bottom of the steering head) was strengthened.

Magneto ignition was first offered as an option. The magneto was situated above the clutch hub and the magneto sprocket was driven by the clutch hub, using the middle row of the new triple-row primary chain. (The triple-row primary chain was also used on battery ignition models.) Introducing a magneto drive opening forced a change in the primary drive chain case and cover. This opening either accommodated the magneto or, in the case of battery ignition models, was

closed by a magneto-drive-opening cover. For racing purposes, riders and tuners favored the 1934 double-row primary drive for the balance of Indian's racing history, because the narrower 1934 primary drive housing gave extra clearance for steeply banked sliding left turns on dirt tracks. The magneto ignition model had a new toolbox because the magneto occupied the earlier toolbox area.

1936 Standard Scout and Sport Scout Highlights

For 1936 Indian designated the larger bike the "Standard Scout" in order to lessen confusion with the Sport Scout. "T" oil lines lubricated the valve guides, which required accommodating changes to the right crankcase. The standard battery ignition used a distributor instead of a wasted-spark circuit breaker. The distributor unit was mounted on the timing case cover and driven by the rear camshaft. This change resulted in spinoff changes to the rear camshaft and the timing case cover. On magneto ignition models, the distributor drive hole was blanked off by a cover plate. Alloy T-slot pistons featured a thickened head, a different beveling of the head edge, reinforced

Now less sought after than the companion Sport Scout, the Scout (renamed the Standard Scout in 1936) was of equal prestige in the mid-1930s. Surprisingly, the Scout (Standard Scout) was always slightly higher priced than the Sport Scout. The optional "V" tank panel was a new offering for the 1935 season, and remained an option through 1939. A restoration error is the primary drive cover, which should have the Indian script.

The Great Ayers Rock Australian Shootout

Kevin Storey and I left Melbourne on a Sunday afternoon, hauling in the back of the Ute (pickup) two perfect Indian Scouts. Seven hours and about 400 miles later we limped into Ouyen with an automatic transmission that was failing. The next day we drove out of Ouyen in the replacement Ute. Our cruising speed was 150 kph,

This 1936 Sport Scout has the new flush-mounted bullet-shaped taillight. The 1936 front fender doesn't have the Indian head ornament. In the background, the Australian outback's Ayers Rock, just 1,825 miles from the author's home "port" in Melbourne!

about 91 mph. After dark, I got a closeup look at a kangaroo. He hopped right into the body panel just behind the passenger door, leaving a big dent. After seven hours of Kevin's driving we arrived in Port Augusta, and bedded down under the stars because the RV park office was closed.

On Tuesday Kevin slowed down from the usual 150 kph cruise to about half that. We were low on gas, er, petrol, and he hoped the slower pace would get us to the next station. Eight kilometers from the Opal mining town of Coober Pedy, the Ute died. Minutes passed with no vehicles approaching.

Bright idea time. Kevin said if we both urinated into the petrol filler our urine would raise the fuel level slightly, the Ute would start, and we could roll into the town just past the two hills. Bladders emptied, and with me silently skeptical, we got in the Ute. It started! But we were able to roll only another mile or two. Another Ute pulled with several Jerry cans of petrol, each worth about $30 Australian. Kevin paid him $50, including what he termed a $20 stupidity tax. The Ute wasn't interested. Diagnosis: urine in the fuel filter. Kevin climbed below and started disconnecting the filter. Suddenly, a face full of urine! In a few minutes, we were again on our way. We covered over a thousand miles that day by the time we arrived at Ayers Rock in the dusk, giving us just a few minutes to scout out possible photo sites.

On Wednesday afternoon, over the course of three hours, I shot five rolls of film at Ayers Rock. Film and time are cheap when you know you can't come back.

Work done, we headed back Thursday morning. There are 1,825 miles between Melbourne and Ayers Rock. We made the return drive to Melbourne in two days, without incident. When we reached Melbourne, we had spent six days and traveled over 3,600 miles mainly to produce just two pictures.

An important Sport Scout attribute was the increased ground clearance over that of the earlier Series 101. This made the Sport Scout a better layout for sliding sideways on America's dirt racetracks. Incidentally, Ayers Rock is the world's largest monolith, standing over 950 feet high and with a perimeter of over 5-1/2 miles.

On the 1936 and 1937 Sport Scouts, Standard Scouts, and Chiefs, two "T" lines fed oil to the front and rear cylinder valve guides. On 1936 battery ignition models, a distributor unit replaced the earlier wasted spark circuit breaker. This tank paint scheme was termed the "Arrow" panel, and was offered on 1935–1939 models. Large quick-action "bayonet" filler caps replaced the earlier small screw-on caps.

Beginning on the 1935 Sport Scouts, provisions were made for magneto ignition via a removable magneto takeoff drive. On battery ignition models like this one, the unused drive was replaced by a cover plate. The 1934 primary drive was via a two-row chain; the 1935 and later primary drive was a triple-row chain, one row being added for magneto drive through a sprocket.

piston pin bosses, and ribbed inside edges. The heavier inlet and exhaust valve springs (same spring for both) were the same as used previously on the Chief only. The right crankcase was fitted with a new sump housing and tube assembly to improve oil pickup.

The fork links were made thicker. Larger tank filler caps featured "bayonet" quick-action instead of screw-on action. The gearshift lever knob was onion shaped instead of ball shaped. This was the first year of fitting a stoplight as a standard feature instead of an accessory. Frame bosses (Scout-right side; Sport Scout-left side) accommodated the switch. The taillight was bullet shaped and mounted flush with the rear fender.

1936 Highlights Unique to the Sport Scout

There was no Indian head ornament on the front fender. The horn was mounted from the center underside instead of from the right and left sides, and thus eliminated were the two mounting tabs on the top center of the fork. The frame shift lever boss was widened from 1-1/2 inches to 3 inches, and the lever hole enlarged from 1/2 inch to 5/8 inch.

1937 Standard Scout and Sport Scout Highlights

1937 marked the last year of the larger model, the Standard Scout. The gearshift lever was moved to the front of the tank, and frame lugs were changed to accommodate. All engines were "Y" type. An optional four-speed transmission was

available. The headlight body didn't have a focusing screw because of the pre-focused lens. The dimmer function was operated by a handlebar-mounted toggle instead of a multi-position switch on the instrument panel. The Standard Scout used a two-piece chain guard and on both the Standard Scout and Sport Scout the chain guard was larger. On the Sport Scout only, the rear fender valance was increased (i.e., became the same as on the Standard Scout and Chief). According to parts books, the optional full-color Indian head tank decor was offered on late-1937 models.

An unpopular change was the introduction of a coarser clutch worm thread in the primary drive cover (clutch worm nut) and on the clutch release worm, which produced a quicker acting clutch. With the motorcycle running, in gear, and with the clutch disengaged, the engine vibration sometimes gradually engaged the clutch.

1938 Sport Scout Highlights

A flush-mounted tank top instrument panel contained the first-ever standard issue speedometer, as well as the ammeter and ignition switch. The instruments had a one-year-only finish of gray background with red needle, numbers, and markings; the speedometer was a 120-miles-per-hour unit. The ignition switch was gray. After the supply of gray switches ran out, a few machines used either a black or an amber switch. Handle grips were gray. Publicity photos showed a gray gearshift knob—no doubt intended—but production models had a black knob. The full-color Indian head tank decor was offered (and may have been offered on late-1937 models). The Indian script on the tank figurehead was offered in see-through (tank-matching) color, and these were offered with either gold or silver silhouette. The fork stem bracket (the casting that interfaced between the steering head and fork top) was larger.

The "T" oil lines were eliminated, but four-piece clamshell valve covers were continued. A larger square oil pump body included the distributor drive, and the right crankcase was changed to accommodate the new pump. The cylinders had larger cooling fins and mated with larger exhaust tubes that were built into a single assembly with the collector tube. A 2-1/8-inch long wiring terminal block was mounted on the rear fender. "Z" metal flywheels were introduced on late-1938 high-performance Daytona motors. The "Z" metal had properties that were a compromise between easily machinable iron and stronger but less machinable steel.

1939 Sport Scout Highlights

Indian offered optional metallic finishes for 1939. Except for silver, this was a first. Small parts,

This circa-1936 Scout hillclimber special has an unusual though not unique inlet-over-exhaust or F-head cylinder layout. This bike's history is unknown. I know of one home-built F-head Scout, which was ridden by Californian Harold Mathewson, but this example appears factory-made.

"except cylinders and those subjected to extreme heat" (Motorcyclist, October 1938) were cadmium plated (previously they had been nickel plated). The headlight lens was larger. A barrel-type fork spring was fitted, and this required a new design consisting of a lower horizontal fork brace with a large threaded boss over which the spring was screwed. "Dog bone" fork damping adjusters replaced disk adjusters. The 1939 fork was offered from February 27 through November 7 as a reduced price retrofit kit for dealers who wished to convert earlier Sport Scouts.

The "World's Fair" optional paint scheme was offered (along with the earlier "V," Arrow, and Plain tank panels). Instruments were black with silver lettering and markings, and the speedometer was a 130-miles-per-hour unit. A circular air cleaner replaced the former arrow-shaped air horn. The tailpipe was upswept. A 2-11/16-inch terminal block was mounted on the rear fender, and a chrome-plated rear fender bumper was fitted.

The "Z" metal flywheels introduced on late-1938 Daytona motors were now standard on all Sport Scouts. The high performance "Bonneville" Sport Scout, successor to the Daytona model, featured connecting rods with a rib around each lower (big end) ring. Other new parts included: pushrod guides, non-trench heads, standard and Bonneville cylinders to mate with the new heads, Bonneville alloy pistons, standard pistons, standard motor

valve collars with two-piece keys, Bonneville motor valve collars with two-piece keys, standard cams, Bonneville cams, Bonneville exhaust valve lifters, sump-valve back plate, four-speed shifter cam, four-speed shifter segment, and gas cap with needle valve and coil spring.

A Trip to the World's Fair—New Motorcycle Concepts Formed

Indian President E. Paul du Pont visited the New York World's Fair in 1939. DuPont took his family by boat and stayed several weeks. While there, he purchased three motorcycles, a Norton single, a BMW, and a Triumph vertical twin. The three motorcycles influenced the design of three forthcoming Indians, the so-called Big Base Scout, the prototype X-44 four cylinder, and the production Model 841 army shaft-drive machine.

A "Real" Racer 1933–1939

"Indian built real racing motorcycles: the Sport Scouts. I passed them in the turns with my Harley, but on the straightaways the Indians took turns going by me." The man talking about the mid-1930s is Harley-Davidson racing star Bennie Campanale, who won the 1938 and 1939 Daytona Beach 200-mile road race and many other premier events.

Facing extinction, the two factories had gotten together in 1932 to design a new class of racing

Somewhere in New England, circa 1939. In the foreground, a "bobbed" 1939 Sport Scout; to its left, a Series 101 Scout "bobber." The 101 Scouts remained popular play bikes long after they went out of production. *Baer family collection*

for the forthcoming 1933 racing season of the A.M.A. It seems too much of a coincidence that Indian set off on the design trail in 1933 to build a motorcycle that just happened to be ideal for the new racing class. Surely the Sport Scout was a purpose-built "real racing motorcycle" disguised as an ordinary road model but ideal for a new class of motorcycle racing.

And what was the new racing class? It was a new "stock" racing game that required riders to own their motorcycles and to ride them to the events. No trailers allowed! More importantly, the new class was limited to standard production or "stock" motorcycles of side-valve (flathead) layout and not more than 45-ci of displacement. These engines were necessarily limited in the compression ratio because of the eccentric combustion chambers, and it was thought that they were beyond the scope of serious tuning efforts. So much the better, since it was the intent of both Indian and Harley-Davidson to extricate themselves from the expense of supporting racing programs.

The Indian 45-ci engine had already demonstrated superior breathing qualities that enabled a carefully tuned Scout to outrun both Harley-Davidson and Indian 74-ci twins. Now this basic engine design was improved with a "Y" inlet manifold and aluminum cylinder heads. Moreover, the "keystone" frame layout, which dispensed with the

twin lower horizontal frame tubes on either side of the powerplant, resulted in greatly increased ground clearance. The Sport Scout could be banked over more steeply than the Series 101 Scout when sliding through flat track corners. The girder fork may or may not have improved typical ordinary road riding, but for racing it offered the advantage of increased travel. This was perhaps not important in flat track racing but was significant in another form of stock racing that later evolved in today's motocross.

The new game was termed "Class C" because there was already Class A for unrestricted, factory-supported racing, and Class B for non-factory riders who were allowed limited modifications to their machines. Almost as an afterthought, Class C permitted the use of 30.50-ci overhead-valve motorcycles. English motorcycles of this size were popular in Canada, but the Canadian motorcycle population was small compared to that of the United States, and the "thirty-fifty" overheads were almost nonexistent in the United States. It was viewed as largely an academic affair, there being only one prominent American dealer in English-built bikes (New York's Reggie Pink). (After World War II, the "mixed-bag" racing rules would become controversial.)

In addition to the Class C mixed bag of 45-ci flatheads and the rarely seen 30.50-ci overheads,

66

there was a big flathead motor class of up to 80-ci. The big bikes were permitted in hillclimbing and "TT" racing, but not in flat-track racing. The American "TT" races were so named because they were inspired by the world-famous Isle of Man Tourist Trophy (or TT) races. Originally dubbed "miniature TT" races, the "miniature" label was soon dropped. These TT races were run over unevenly textured surfaces, in contrast to flat-track races, which were deceptively simple in appearance. Actually, building a good flat-track course was complicated by the need for a uniform track surface and a "tacky" composition such as clay that would increase speeds, minimize slide out, and minimize dust. Additionally, flat-track layout required careful surveying and grading to achieve banking that was not excessive, yet facilitated rapid runoff of rainwater. Since local motorcycle clubs were active in race promotion, the TT events were more in keeping with their amateur

Above: The brilliant maroon and orange paint scheme was a standard no-extra-charge option. The green pinstriping was unique, as all other Indian standard striping was in gold. The new cylinders had larger cooling fins. A larger square oil pump featured an integral distributor drive. "T" oil lines were omitted, but four-piece "clam shell" valve covers continued.

Above, left: Indian followed Harley-Davidson's styling lead and used a tank top instrument panel in lieu of an exposed speedometer body. This was the first year Indian provided a speedometer as standard equipment. The attractive gray-and-red instruments were a 1938-only feature.

Left: The years 1938 and 1939 saw Indian styling at its peak in the open-fender era. The 1938 engines were the last to run with an air deflector instead of an air cleaner. This also was the first year in which there was no Standard Scout offered alongside the Sport Scout.

No Indian motorcycle is more famous than this 1939 Sport Scout campaigned by the legendary Ed Kretz Sr. in 1939 and the early and late 1940s. The bike was a cunningly built "cheater." The special frame was built of chrome moly steel. The front cylinder nearly touches the front down tube because the powerplant has been tilted forward. This raised the clutch hub section of the primary drive compartment, giving Kretz needed additional ground clearance for sliding on steeply banked dirt tracks.

construction skills and limited finances. All a TT course required was a clear path around the course; the rougher and more irregular, the better. The rules stipulated at least one left turn, at least one right turn, and at least one jump, the last inspired by dramatic Isle of Man photos of leaping bikes soaring over arched bridges.

Class C racing debuted in the 1933 season, somewhat as an experiment. Meanwhile, all-out Class A racing continued without strong factory support, but in the hands of an increasingly smaller cadre of riders left over from the pre-World War I era of big factory teams. For some years, Class A flat-track racing had been limited to special single-cylinder 21.35-ci (350-cc) Indians and Harley-Davidsons. These singles weren't representative of what Americans rode, and lacked the audible "potato, potato" charm of the V-twins, which along with the dwindling race rider corps contributed to lessened appeal.

In setting up Class C racing, the factories had not considered establishing national championship events, because the "nationals" were viewed

This historic motorcycle is the sole surviving prewar big-base Scout. This bike features the large streamlined cylinders and heads introduced on 1940 models, and the vertically mounted magneto layout which was introduced in 1948. Kretz chromed the fork and frame in the late 1940s.

Riding a Sport Scout

From my *Indian Buyer's Guide*, originally published in 1989, here's my unchanged impression of riding an Indian Sport Scout:

You fire up the motor and it makes an angry sound despite the muffler. You blip the throttle, but the motor is a little cold natured and it stutters. You set the throttle for a fast steady idle for a minute. Some more throttle twisting and the engine responds eagerly. A little higher on the next blip, and still higher on the next, and on the third you let the revs soar for just an instant. The motor says let's get on with it, and you begin to get the racer feel. You close your eyes to see more clearly. This is the 1938 Springfield (Illinois) mile, and you're the world's greatest flat-tracker about to defeat the Harley gang. Eyes open again. In gear and away. No time to spend running slow—that's not the forte of a Sport Scout. Head for a fast road and wind it up in low. It sings. Shift to second at 25 miles per hour and more high notes. Shift to high at 50 and roar on up to 75—there's more there but you don't want to take a chance with your friend's treasure, so you back off to 70. You look down at the engine. Yeah, it's a side-valve all right. Doesn't seem possible. Feels like a double overhead cam—it loves to rev. The exhaust resonates. One word sums up the Sport Scout: Wild.

as something to be escaped rather than re-created. Thus, Class C races and hill climbs were local matters during 1933. Class C was a boon to the sport because it got local dealers more involved in the racing game. Those dealers and mechanics who had been sharpening their flathead tuning skills in the Indian-versus-Harley street wars now found an official outlet for their abilities. There was also the matter of dealers recruiting new Class C riders because the old corps of Class A insiders had a hammerlock on special equipment. Recruitment built enthusiasm, and enthusiasm built recruitment. Class C popularity grew at an unpredictable pace. The first Class C national championship races, a six-hour endurance race and a 200-mile TT, were held in July 1934, and both were won by Harley riders! But the Indian Sport Scout would soon reign supreme.

One of the hotshot dealer/tuners was Roland "Rollie" (rhymes with holy) Free of Indianapolis, Indiana. Free recalls:

We kept working on Indians to increase speed and rapidly became a thorn in Harley-Davidson sales. We developed a 45-cubic-inch side-valve Indian [Sport Scout] and a rider, Rody Rodenburg, who was undefeated for 3-1/2 years and had a string of 38 straight first places and 14 track records on half-mile dirt tracks sanctioned by the American Motorcycle Association. We were very lucky as we had no breakdowns in any of these races.

Rodenburg was the first Indian rider to win a Class C national championship race, the 200-mile road race at Jacksonville, Florida, held in February 1935. In September, "Woodsie" Castonguay of Indian's hometown of Springfield, Massachusetts, won the 100-mile national championship on the steeply banked one-mile egg-shaped dirt track. "Speedway" was the American term given to such long steeply banked dirt tracks (but the egg-shape wasn't required). Not only did Castonguay win that race, but Indians finished second, third, fifth, sixth, and seventh places.

By 1936, Indian and Harley-Davidson were heavily advertising all Class C victories and the sport was beginning a subtle transition into a variant of the dwindling old Class A game. Top riders were conveniently employed as wrench turners by dealers. The shop-employed riders enjoyed the advantage of working on their own motorcycles with a full slate of the shop's equipment, and theoretically on the riders' own time. Such double-barreled racer-employee status also provided

Circa 1936: Rider Ted Edwards demonstrated his racing posture at Daytona Beach, Florida. The bike sports several Indian racing accessories, including front fender, exhaust system, and foot "spuds" (pegs). The motorcycle is fitted with a non-standard "T" oil line servicing the inlet valves on both cylinders (but not the exhaust valves as on stock 1936–1937 Models.)

Some 101 Scouts were full-time play bikes. This one looks like a "field meet" special, sans front fender and headlight. Lots of 101 Scouts were practically ridden into the ground before being discarded. *Baer family collection*

ample opportunity for using shop time to work on race bikes, which in effect amounted to professional factory-through-dealer racing support. This was contrary to the spirit and the letter of "poor boy" Class "C" racing, which was supposed to be all about eliminating factory and quasi-factory sponsorship. Routine bits and pieces were undoubtedly donated by the dealers, which was yet another rules violation. Although the Class C rules forbade it, both factories either gave or sold at cost significant parts such as cylinders, crankshafts, valves, and so forth. These under-the-table benefits couldn't be traced because of the melding of riders and dealerships, and besides, neither Indian nor Harley supporters wanted to blow the whistle lest they risk their own efforts being halted. In other words, the Olympian ideal had been quickly replaced by a new all-out rivalry between Indian and Harley-Davidson.

Indian was fortunate to enlist the services of Ed Kretz, through Los Angeles dealer Floyd Clymer who hired him as a mechanic. In January 1936, Kretz won the 200-mile national championship

road race at Savannah, Georgia, over a course made from ground-up oyster shells. Class C racing was both dangerous and frivolous. Following the race, Kretz, third-place Indian rider Al Chasteen, and companions answered the Wigwam's invitation and drove to Springfield, Massachusetts. Along the way the boys sideswiped another car, forcing them to wire a door shut. It was the dead of winter in the northeast, and though the heater was kept on full force, the guys had to wrap themselves in blankets. In Washington, D.C., they got lost while driving and unintentionally lapped the city twice. At the Indian factory, all the gals fell in love with the handsome Kretz. Chasteen had his share of female admirers, too, and boosted his prestige by telling some of them that he was Kretz. The Wigwam replaced their damaged door, and the contingent started the long drive back across North America to California.

In April 1936 former Class A rider Fred Ludlow rode a Sport Scout to the amazing speed of 128.57 miles per hour at the Muroc Dry Lake speed trials in the Southern California desert. These speed trials were conducted in one direction only, and the course was set up to benefit from the strong wind. The Sport Scout could be fitted with a smaller rear sprocket than possible with the Indian Chief, which was a key to the spectacular speed. This was not a Class C event, so special fuel and mechanical modifications would have been permitted. The Langhorne 100 was again won by a Sport Scout rider, this time Lester Hillbish, and Indians filled six of the first 10 places. In preparing for the race, rider Howard Mitzel made an interesting discovery. He eliminated the characteristic heart shape (or Mickey Mouse shape) from the combustion chamber by grinding away the raised area between the valves, producing a skull shape instead. The improved high-speed breathing more than compensated for the lower compression ratio.

In June 1936, Rody Rodenburg was credited with a new transcontinental record, having crossed on a Sport Scout in 71 hours and 20 minutes, despite getting off course and traveling about

Except for silver, which was offered in the early 1930s, the year 1939 saw the first offering of metallic finishes—Cascade blue and, as seen here, Sand taupe (with Chinese red panels). The paint scheme, new for 1939, was termed the "World's Fair" style; earlier "plain," "Arrow," and "V" tank panels continued to be available. Other styling touches included the upswept tailpipe and the chrome rear bumper.

71

Since the Series 101 Scout days, Indian had offered a three-wheeled 45-ci model termed the Dispatch Tow. Three-wheelers enjoyed modest success in some cities where they were used by service garages as automobile pickup vehicles. The rider would arrive on the three-wheeler, then use a universal quickly attachable/detachable bumper hitch to tow the three-wheeler back to the garage. After the car was serviced, it was driven back with the three-wheeler in tow, the bike and hitch were then disconnected, and the service man rode the cycle back to work.

300 miles more than he should have. But his local Indian dealer, Rollie Free, recalls that Rodenburg had cheated by towing the bike. In a colossal blunder, says Free, Rodenburg could have made some "real" money by being honest and taking credit for a new automobile record! Free claims to have known nothing about the effort until it had been accomplished, and I know Free to be honest to the extreme.

In January 1937, Kretz and his friend Harrison Reno made the transcontinental drive from California to Daytona Beach, to enter the Daytona 200. As at Savannah the year before, the weekend was also another party. On Saturday night before the next day's 200-miler, Kretz and Reno visited campfires on the beach, roasted wieners, and drank beer. Impromptu motorcycle

drag races were running up and down the beach to settle bets of a few dollars. Kretz and Reno decided to have fun and make some extra money by using their race bikes and challenging all comers. This was an era when about half the motorcycles in a long race would drop out, the victims of this or that mechanical problem. So Kretz and Reno were putting extra stress on their race bikes, perhaps robbing them of a few laps of endurance in tomorrow's big race. The next day, Ed Kretz won the first Daytona 200 despite having fallen. This was Indian's third consecutive 200-mile road race national championship. Kretz's average speed was 74.10 miles per hour over a course that amounted to two drag (sprint) races connected by two treacherous turns in deep sand. Kretz's forte was his ability to charge

through the sandy corners fast, while there were numerous spills among slower riders. The trick was to enter the deep sand under full power, and to never slow down in the turns. While this may have been understood by some other riders, there was for them a gap between understanding and executing. And what of Reno? While running near the front of the pack, his dragster-turned-racer quit after 168 miles.

In June 1937, Lester Hillbish found himself at the 100-mile New England TT Championship with a sick racing motorcycle.. In a throwback to the original Class C rules, Hillbish borrowed a Sport Scout that had been ridden 550 miles to the event, stripped the Sport Scout of front fender, lights, and other road gear, then won the race! In

August, Hillbish also won the most prestigious of flat-track races, the Springfield, Illinois, 25-mile national championship for 1-mile tracks. September saw Kretz win the 100-mile Langhorne title, Indian's third consecutive for that event, with an average speed of 82.1 miles per hour. Kretz was able to ride the entire egg-shaped course without shutting off—full throttle all the way through the turns. Fellow Indian rider Ted Edwards asked Kretz how he had the nerve to go so fast through the corners, and Kretz replied that it wouldn't hurt any more to fall at 90 miles per hour than at 85 miles per hour!

Also in 1937, news of an under-the-table match race win was happily circulated among the Indian dealer network. Harley-Davidson TT star

On the 1939 Sport Scouts, fork "dog bone" damping adjusters replaced disk adjusters. A circular air cleaner replaced the former arrow-shaped air horn. Small parts except those subject to extreme heat (e.g., cylinders) were cadmium plated instead of nickel plated.

The large oil pump was introduced on 1938 models. Two-piece screw-on valve covers were again used—the first since 1935.

J.B. Jones of Marion, Indiana, had been racing the very Harley used by factory rider Joe Petrali to set a Class C record of 102.047 miles per hour at Daytona Beach. Indianapolis Indian dealer Rollie Free goaded Jones into the match race (straight-away, for highest top speed) by boasting in front of a large crowd, "I can beat the Harley beach record with my wife on back of the machine-double."

After being trounced by about 10 miles per hour, Jones offered to match race his Harley 80 against Free's Indian 74. Free responded: "I won't even bother to go get the Chief. I'll just run my Scout against your 80. You want to bring your 80 out now?" Jones didn't.

American motorcycle racing of the era was perhaps the only sport in which the annual season began with the most prestigious of all events, the Daytona 200. In January 1938, Harley-Davidson rider Ben Campanale won the Daytona classic. But before the rest of the racing season got under way in the spring, Indian again grabbed headlines. Rollie Free set Class C 74- and 45-ci records of 109.65 (Chief) and 111.55 miles per hour. Having the Sport Scout outrun the Chief was a bit embarrassing to Indian, but both marks were well above Harley-Davidson's previous marks of 105-plus (Muroc Dry Lake, special fuel) for a 74-ci model, and 102.047 (Daytona, Class C) for a 45-ci model. The slower speed with the 74-ci Chief was caused by "wet sumping," that is, failure of crankcase oil to be quickly returned to the oil tank. By June, Indian held every Class C record for dirt-track races on half-mile flat tracks.

In August, Woodsie Castonguay won the 25-mile national championship at Springfield, Illinois, with an average speed of 78.8 miles per hour. The seven fastest qualifiers were all Indian mounted, and though Ed Kretz failed to qualify, he set a 10-mile record in a consolation race for non-qualifiers. In September, Kretz won the inaugural Laconia national championship race, termed a TT and run for 200 miles. It was this grueling race, finished in the hours of approaching darkness, that earned him the nickname "Iron Man." The bigger-is-slower speed record embarrassment was removed in September at Bonneville Salt Flats, Utah, when Fred Ludlow reached 115.126 miles per hour on a Sport Scout and 120.747 miles per hour on a Chief. At season's end, Woodsie Castonguay was termed the "national dirt track champion" by *Motorcyclist* magazine on the basis of his season-long performance. Indian riders also held 8 of the 12 Class C records at year-end, and Ed Kretz was voted the most popular rider in the nation by the hundreds of A.M.A. clubs. The 1938 season had started with the disappointing Harley-Davidson victory in the Daytona 200, but in overall achievement, Indian had enjoyed its best year of Class C racing. Incidentally, due to the popularity of Class C competition, Class A racing was discontinued at the end of the year.

In 1939, Harley-Davidson star Ben Campanale again won the biggest prize, the Daytona 200. But the balance of the year favored Indian. In April 1939, Bob Hallowell raced a 45-ci Sport Scout and won the 80-ci TT national championship at Chattanooga, Tennessee. In May, Woodsie Castonguay set two new half-mile track records at Richmond, Virginia, en route to winning his preliminary (heat) race and the 10-mile feature event. Indian again held every record for half-mile flat tracks, with Woodsie owning three records and his brother Frenchy owning the other. At the same race meet, Indian riders Freddy Toscani and Lester Hillbish joined Woodsie in under-30-second lap times, marking the first time in Class C history that under-30-second times had been made on a half-mile track. On August 19, Indian won the 25-mile national championship at Springfield, Illinois, for the third consecutive time, the winner being Stanley Wittinski, with second place going to Indian rider Lester Hillbish. A week later, the first 50-mile dirt-track national championship in 17 years was held on the Syracuse, New York, one-mile track. Indian rider Lester Hillbish won and four other Indian riders rounded out the top five. At season's end, Indian owned 11 of 14 track records, including all four half-mile track records and four out of six one-mile track records.

To sum it up, Indian dominated Class C national championship racing of the 1930s. However, Harley-Davidson showed increasing

strength late in the decade. Indian must have felt it got its hard-earned money's worth from their Sport Scout design work of 1933, a gamble the Wigwam had taken at the very bottom of the Great Depression and with no assurance that the bottom had yet been reached. Although Harley-Davidson continuously outsold Indian two to one, the Sport Scout had carried the Indian banner proudly, managing to win the majority of the national championships. In the process, the Sport Scout had become the soul of Indian. From Harley-Davidson comes perhaps the most authoritative praise of the Sport Scout. After traveling over the nation visiting Harley-Davidson dealers, junior executive William H. Davidson (later, company president) filed a report in October 1936. After noting the many Indian racing victories, young Davidson reported that the Sport Scout "seemed to be a better job than ours."

Roland "Rollie" Free at Daytona Beach, March 17, 1938. Free set a new 45-ci Class C (stock) record of 111.55 miles per hour. Once, when negotiating a bet on a top-speed race with a Harley-Davidson rider, the Harley rider didn't offer to put any money up front, explaining "It's a gentleman's bet." Free retorted, "I've never had a gentleman's bet with a Harley guy in my life!" *Rollie Free collection*

75

Chapter Five

The Streamliners:
1940–1942

Dramatically restyled Indians ushered in a new era. Revolutionary skirted fenders and a full-coverage chain guard graced all Indian models. Although universally popular among today's collectors, the skirted fenders were controversial in their day. Frank Christian, a mechanic at Floyd Clymer's Los Angeles agency, recalls that he could hardly wait for the new skirted fender models to arrive. Max Bubeck, a respected Indian rider in speed trials and cross-country runs, opines, "That's when Indian quit making motorcycles and started making Harleys."

For 1940, Indian gave the skirted fender treatment to all models, even to the low-cost little twin, which they renamed the "Thirty-Fifty" (meaning 30.50 ci).

1940 Sport Scout Highlights

Many of the following features were incorporated on the big twin Chief and/or the inline Four. Continuing the more streamlined theme were new cylinders and cylinder heads that some riders retrofitted to their earlier Sport Scouts. Early-season cylinders had a round base but later production switched to square based cylinders. The fork was 1/2 inch longer and 1/8 inch wider, the latter to accommodate the new front fender. A tab on each lower fork leg secured the skirts. New tanks included metal teardrop emblems. Bonded rubber footboards were level. On the battery ignition model, the coil was on the rear fender (instead of beneath the left tank). Early publicity photos didn't show it, but a wraparound air cleaner was standard equipment. A "Fill-Rite" battery eased servicing. Two-color finishes may have been offered as extra-cost options.

Early-season transmission covers had an oil filler plug for the transmission because it was sealed off from the separately oiled primary drive case and clutch. Later transmission covers didn't have the filler plug, and the transmission reverted to sharing a common oil supply with the primary drive and clutch. For the first time, a centerstand was fitted. The centerstand was maintained in the riding (up) position by a latch. A cast-in lower rear frame section replaced the earlier cross tube. The sidestand was standard issue instead of an accessory. The new toolbox was mounted vertically, above the primary cover and in front of the battery. A new one-piece exhaust system was fitted.

This was the first year that Indians were equipped with Linkert carburetors instead of Schebler units. Linkert had bought Schebler several years earlier, and new Harley-Davidsons had used the Linkert label since 1934. Whether bearing the Schebler or Linkert label in this era, the functional differences between Indian and Harley-Davidson carburetors were based on particular models' needs and not on fundamental differences

The year 1940 saw new skirted fender styling debut. "Style blazers of a new era in motorcycling . . . a new and modern trend in motorcycle appearance," proclaimed *Indian News*, the company's periodic rider newsletter. This 1940 Sport Scout is finished in Jade green. The new larger streamlined cylinders and heads were retrofitted to many earlier models by approving riders.

in engineering approach. The Linkert and Schebler carburetors were practically identical in appearance. Edison-Splitdorf magnetos on the Sport Scout (and Chief) were of the new rotating magnet (RM) design with a more rectangular external shape. (The RM magneto had debuted a year before on the Indian Four as an option to battery ignition.) From May 27 through November 7, the RM magnetos were offered as a reduced-price retrofit item for dealers who wished to convert earlier models. A soft rubber distributor cover was a one-year-only feature, but the cover was offered for a while thereafter as an accessory item. The generator end cap cover was cadmium plated instead of black.

A Purolater oil filter was mounted above the clutch pedal. The filter could easily be installed backwards, which slowed oil flow, sometimes blew up the filter, and caused an accumulation of debris around the sump screen and in the oil pump. Even when installed properly, when hot motors cooled off in freezing weather the resulting condensation would freeze the filters closed. Consequently, in midseason the filter was eliminated.

1940 Thirty-fifty Highlights

For 1940, Indian renamed the little twin the "Thirty-fifty," signifying its 30.50-ci displacement (as always). Changes included: skirted fenders, new fork with all straight tubes, and provisions for new fender and new headlight pedestal, larger tanks, compression saddle springs, rubber distributor cover, Linkert carburetor, circular fuse block, bonded rubber footboards, new "Fill-Rite" battery, new toolbox mounted at the lower right front of the rear fender, and new exhaust pipes and muffler.

Out for a little fun on his 1941 Sport Scout. Most Indian enthusiasts who rode double preferred the larger Chief to the Sport Scout. Performance of the heavy-skirted fender Sport Scouts was mild, especially when riding double.
Bill Brown collection

Circa 1940: Young Louise Scherbyn on one of her many well-publicized tours. She had her 1940 Thirty-Fifty custom-painted white by her local dealer. This bike has a unique claim: it's the most photographed motorcycle in *Indian News*, having appeared several times over the years.

1940 Racing Parity with Harley-Davidson

Entering the 1940 racing season, Indian held 11 of 14 Class C racing records. Unfortunately, rider Babe Tancrede gave Harley-Davidson its third consecutive Daytona 200 win. This was American racing's biggest prize. Indian rider Ted Edwards won a couple of TT nationals on a Chief. Melvin Rhoades rode a Sport Scout to the 25-mile national championship on the one-mile track in Springfield, Illinois. This was Indian's fourth consecutive win in arguably the most prestigious of the nation's one-mile flat-track races. The other style of long dirt track was the steeply banked and heavily oiled "speedway." Indian and Harley-Davidson split the two national speedway titles. Indian's Ed Kretz took the Langhorne 100, Indian's sixth consecutive victory in this national, but Louis Guanella won the 200-mile national on the Oakland speedway. Harley-Davidson's Babe Tancrede won the Laconia 100-mile road race national.

In assessing Indian's performance in the 1940 Daytona 200, these facts stood out: in addition to finishing in 1st place, Harleys also finished 3rd, 4th, 5th, 6th, 7th, 9th, and 10th. Indian stars failing to finish included Frenchy Castonguay, Ted Edwards, Art Hafer, Jimmy Kelly, Ed Kretz, Johnny Spiegelhoff, and Stanley Wittinski. The results were even worse in the Oakland 200, in which Harleys took the first seven places. Only one Indian Sport Scout ridden by Mario Stillo finished the complete 200 miles. It was clear that the Sport Scouts weren't holding up in the 200-milers. Something had to be done.

1941 Sport Scout Highlights

Heading this list of new features on the 1941 Sport Scout was the addition of a spring frame similar to the one introduced the previous year on the Chief and Four. The chrome-plated sealed-beam headlight was mounted on a new pedestal and the wiring was routed through the pedestal instead of just the headlight shell. A new horn proclaimed "INDIAN" in block letters, and there was no Indian head design. The horn had a round back instead of a flat back. New handle grips were of uniform diameter and were used for the balance of Indian production. The oil cap was embossed with the word "OIL."

The sales literature described two-color finishes that were available as standard no-extra-cost options (two-color paint schemes may have been

A nice touch to the 1940 Thirty-Fifty was the integrated fender and rear chain guard. Skirted fenders were a one-year-only feature of the 1940 Thirty-Fifty. The new fork was closely patterned after the Sport Scout unit. On the Thirty-Fifty, there were only two color choices: Fallon brown as seen here, or Seafoam blue.

Indian fitted the 1941 Sport Scouts with a plunger rear suspension. Other new touches included a chrome-plated sealed beam headlight and decorative chrome tank strips. Since its inception in 1934, the Sport Scout had grown from 385 pounds to 500 pounds. Performance of road models had thus become a bit underwhelming. However, this example is configured to Bonneville specifications, and if the rider extends open-throttle operation through first and second gears, the engine pulls strongly at near racing revolutions.

offered on 1940 models as extra-cost options). A 5.00x16 tire was available as an option. Decorative strips were placed on the tanks, a short one in front of the Indian emblem and a long one behind the emblem. Incidentally, the 1941 sales catalog was printed too early to include this feature in the illustrations. In the tank top instrument panel, a 110-miles-per-hour speedometer replaced the previous 130-miles-per-hour unit. Additional saddle padding was provided. The toolbox was mounted on the left rear fender skirt and was painted in the same color as the fender skirt.

New pistons were two ounces lighter than previous pistons. The factory provided new balancing instructions. The transmission main shaft

and sprocket driver gear were lengthened 3/4 inch to accommodate the new wider frame needed for the coil spring suspension units.

1941 Thirty-Fifty Highlights

The thirty-fifty front and rear fenders changed to a new open style. The tank trim was changed from the Indian head and large Indian script to a teardrop transfer that mimicked the large models' metal emblem.

Who Got the Big Base "Cheaters"?

I accept Stephen du Pont's recollections as the sole-surviving on-the-scene participant. Over the decades, memories diverged. Although Steve

continued on page 87

A nifty Sport Scout bobber from the 1940s in California. *Chuck Otis collection*

Above: Here, we see a Fallon brown and Kashan green 1941 Sport Scout, which would have been an extra-cost option. The 1941 standard-cost one-color finishes were black, Brilliant red, and Seafoam blue. Standard two-color finishes included combinations of these, such as red fender skirts, chain guard, and toolbox, with white fender centers and tanks. Riders willing to pay an extra fee could basically choose any combinations of any available Indian colors from current or previous years.

Right: The Sport Scout engines of the era are among the more attractive ever designed for motorcycle use. It's hard to imagine how the aesthetics could be improved in any way.

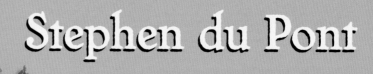

Stephen du Pont

of the pump through the crankshaft and the connecting rod bearings, and the oil then exited as a mist into the crankcase, whereupon it was slung by the flywheels, connecting rods, and crankshaft. The slung oil lubricated the cylinder walls and cooled the case and the moving parts. The oil mist then fell like rain into a built-in pocket or "sump" at the bottom of the case. From the sump, the oil was sucked out by the pump mechanism. The return mechanism in the pump was designed to have several times the flow capacity of the supply pump because it was important that excess oil not gather in the crankcase. At normal road speeds, the supply and return capabilities were in balance. There was one continuous process of delivery, lubrication, cooling, and recovery.

But in the longer and faster races such as the Daytona 200, the engines proved incapable of sucking oil fast enough from the sump. The resulting buildup of oil in the crankcase produced higher and higher pressures that increasingly resisted the delivery of additional oil by the supply pump. The crankcase pressure eventually became so high that it prohibited the constant flow of sufficient oil through the crankshaft and the connecting rod bearings into the crankcase. The situation became a paradox, in that while the crankcase contained too much oil, the vital connecting rod bearings became oil starved! The excess crankcase oil also acted like a hydraulic brake, robbing the engine of its full output. The problem, then, was to supply more oil to the connecting rod bearings but less oil to the crankcase. A two-pronged course was undertaken: one, to increase the delivery of the supply pump, and two, to suck oil out faster from the crankcase so that the net result would be an optimum crankcase supply (less oil than in the unmodified engines).

Stephen du Pont was E. Paul du Pont's third of six sons. While Stephen was studying at the Massachusetts Institute of Technology (M.I.T.) in 1937, Indian built an experimental single-cylinder swash-plate research airplane engine for M.I.T. professor Alfaro. This is cited as an example of the technical interest and capabilities of Paul du Pont and his Indian company. Shortly afterwards, Stephen and his next-older brother George joined the Indian sales department. Stephen was soon transferred to the engineering department, whose staff included Gus Hasbrouk, who later became a famous engineer for Pratt and Whitney aircraft engines. Before getting into motorcycle work, Stephen's first job was to layout assembly drawings for a flathead horizontally opposed auxiliary power unit (A.P.U.) for a Martin flying boat. In short, the Indian engineering department was producing state-of-the-art designs. Nothing less would be expected of young Stephen when he was given the job of making racing Sport Scouts stay together in long events like the Daytona 200.

Indian Lubrication

Before discussing the engineering efforts that produced the first so-called "Big Base" Sport Scouts, here's an overview of how the dry-sump (circulating) lubrication system worked. Oil was forced by the supply portion

Engineering the Prewar Big Base Scouts
as told by Stephen du Pont

We now take up the story as told by Stephen du Pont of the Indian engineering department.

About that time I had inherited the job in the experimental department in the Indian factory of trying to make the big ends stay in the 45-ci Bonneville racers for the long 200-mile races. Many kinds of bearings had been tried, and there was a drawer of them all black and stuck together. Jim Taylor, bless his soul, a wonderful man, was running the experimental department and I talked to him about it. His idea was simply that we couldn't get enough oil to the bearing.

I went down into the factory and got a set of gears for the Indian Four gear oil pump, and we removed the plunger pump and drove the gear pump off the lower end of the distributor shaft. But at high speeds, the pump put in too much oil and the flywheels picked it up and carried it around inside the crankcase, creating a sort of hydraulic brake which heated up the oil, but worse, put a big load on the engine. I wanted to limit the oil flow at the higher speed used in racing, and talked to several people in the factory who knew more than I did about hydraulics, but came up with nothing.

But because of the flywheels picking up oil, we still couldn't get enough oil for the big end connecting rod bearings. Well, my brother Jacques and I had bought a Norton ES-2 from the New York auto show. I took it apart and found it had a scraper at the flywheels that scraped the oil off and dumped it into a sump so the scavenging pump could suck it out.

We sneaked sheet-metal scrapers into the crankcase, aligned with the flywheels, and made a sheet-metal dam to hold the scraped-off oil so the sump pump could get it. Then, the problem was that at cruise rpms it worked fine but at racing rpm speeds we still pumped in too much oil to get out.

What was happening was that when you suck through a large hole there comes a demand for extra flow that the pump can't produce. That is, the oil won't flow that fast through the big hole, and the sump pump is pulling nothing—not even air—pulling nothing—a vacuum. And above that speed you don't increase the flow even though you speed up the gear suction pump.

So I made a plug in the suction pipe and drilled a small hole in it so the sump pump had to suck through that small hole. We set up a pump on the bench with a motor driving it at the rpm used in high-speed racing at Daytona, and played around with various-sized suction orifices. When we found a size that limited the flow about the rpm we had in mind, we put one on the test engine on the dynamometer.

The rollers were a quarter inch around, 5/16-inch long as I remember it, and they were carried in a steel retainer that was a steel ring, having quarter-inch holes bored in from one end, breaking out at the inner and outer diameters. These were heavy, and at 6,000 rpm obviously put a big centrifugal force load on the rollers, acting like a brake and creating a lot of heat. We tried the cast-bronze bearing retainers from the sidecar wheel

bearings, but these also were heavy and were no better, and they broke. I wanted something lighter, and we made some out of aluminum. These broke, cracking in the bottom of the pocket.

Mr. Voorhees from the Aluminum Company of America came into the factory on some other business, and my Dad, E. Paul du Pont, and I took him to lunch. I took up the problem with him and he suggested that the bottom of the roller pocket might have sharp corners, and this would start a failure. So we made some with carefully rounded corners in the bottom of the pocket, and of course had to chamfer the corners of the rollers 1/16 of inch to clear the radius. It figures that 15 rollers would go around the 1-inch crank pin with a little clearance, and to allow for the retainers, as I recall it, we used 10 rollers per roll. There were four rows in the two connecting rods, so that made 40 rollers per big end in an engine. At the time, we had a lot of special parts made outside and making this aluminum retainer was very difficult because the end mill cutter had to break out of the inner and outer diameters of the retainer ring. I finally found a man who could make them. He was Walter O'Conner, who had a machine shop and ran a seaplane base in Agawam, Massachusetts, near Springfield, and took care of my Monocoupe airplane.

We made up six engines with these oil pumps and they went into the Daytona 200-mile race. These engines had a faked casting on the cam cover side to accommodate the new gear pump, and they had scrapers. So they were not Class C because Class C had to be production. Ed Kretz, Teddy Edwards, and at least one of the Castonguays [and] three other riders had these engines, and at the Daytona race they strictly went like hades. Putting in more oil let the big ends hold up the first time in history for the Daytona 200, on the beach and down the road. So, at 180 miles, more or less, everyone was way ahead of the Harleys.

During the race, I was walking with my late friend Bob Nields along the beach when one of the cylinders broke in half; we were walking where the race was being run. A piston flew out of one of the engines which was passing us at about 100 miles an hour, and a man reached down to pick it up. My friend thought that I would want the piston, so he stepped on the man's hand to keep him from picking up the piston. The thing was hotter than the hinges of hades, and the man let out a holler and jumped back. Bob picked up the piston real quick and dropped it into his jacket pocket. The man with the burned hand didn't object.

Then—kapow!—the other cylinders started to break in half! None of them finished! (It was) fatigue failure because we had never been able to run such power and that long at that rpm. This is also the reason the cylinders of the 45 Scout were made square instead of round after the race, to add extra material for strength.

So, I admit 60 years later that I got my comeuppance for this illegal design in Class C, because of the new power and rpm, and none of the six engines survived the race! Amen!

Indian ditched the skirted fenders on the 1941 Thirty-Fifty. These open fenders were the same as used in 1940, minus the skirts. This is a near one-year-only model. At least 31 1942 Thirty-Fifty models were built, as confirmed by motor number EDB131 in Australia.

The rather Harley-like sheet metal-covered primary chain wasn't typical of long-standing Indian practice. Likewise the isolated gearbox mounted to the frame. These items were basically carryovers from the 1925–1928 single-cylinder Prince.

Don't let the silver/gray paint fool you. Indian made the 1938–1942 Thirty-Fifty crankcases and transmission (gearbox) cases out of iron! Another cost-cutting technique was to build the little twin in one color only and to crate them for shipment without any accessories. This avoided time-consuming administration of the custom orders that were typical of the other Indian models.

Continued from page 82
knew of six Big Base engines, the late Erle "Pop" Armstrong (of the service department) remembered only five. Pop passed on his recollections to his son Jack:

> They gave one to Ed Kretz; one to Teddy Edwards; one to Johnny Spieglehoff; one to Stanley Wittinski; and one to Lester Hillbish. Lester blew his, in 1941, and the factory wasn't too happy, so they didn't give him another one. The one that Wittinski had shifted back and forth from Wittinski to Woodsie Castonguay. I think Woodsie used it at Springfield, Illinois, that year. So when the war came on, and they called these motors back into the factory, there were only four, one being blown. They didn't make any spare parts; the casting of the bases was just too expensive. So they called the four back in.

1941 Racing—No More Indian Magic

The 1941 Daytona 200 was won by Canadian Billy Matthews on an overhead-cam Norton single. In a way, the Norton victory was lucky for Indian, because Harley-Davidsons filled all the other positions from 2 through 10 and 12 through 18! Instead of embarrassing Harley-Davidson magazine advertisements that would have come with a Harley victory, there were no advertisements at all because Norton had no presence in the American market. The Wigwam's top finisher was 10th-place man Al Wolfe. The Springfield, Illinois, mile-track remained Indian's property, with Frenchy Castonguay taking the tribe's fifth consecutive 25-mile national championship. Indian's hold on Class C racing records fell from 11 of 14 to 9 of 14.

The 1940–1941 streamlined cylinders and heads immediately found favor among racers like Canadian Romeo Masse of Montreal. Masse used Junior Scout tanks on his bike, in common with many other Indian racers who favored the smaller tanks. The little "cow bell" exhaust funnels were the rage. *Baer family collection*

Another Sport Scout bobber of the California 1940s, its rider not at all concerned about decibels. *Scholfield collection*

The Daytona Beach 200-mile National Championship road race was America's premier motorcycle race from 1937 on. The riders drew their starting positions from a hat and were flagged away at 10-second intervals. (The telephoto lens has compressed the distances between starting rows.) *Baer family collection*

Harley-Davidson's first-ever all-out racing model, the 1941 WR, was a subtle compliment to Indian. Remember the "happy combination," the 1927 45-ci Scout that Indian designed quickly and cheaply, the engine that seemed to work better than it should have? Over the past few years, the Milwaukee brand had progressed closer and closer to the Indian idea (or accident), by moving the valves closer to the cylinder bore. Harley-Davidson did this by inclining the valves (as viewed from the front or rear of the engine) toward the cylinder bores. At long last, racing parity had arrived.

Another prestigious race was the Oakland, California, 200-mile Speedway National Championship. Oakland was a fast and dangerous track. A major pileup in the 1941 race killed two riders and ended another's career, so the event was not renewed after the war. Although the two Sport Scouts are pre-1940, the picture is known to be either from the 1940 or the 1941 race. *Scholfield collection*

Ouch! A Sport Scout rider loses it on a California half-mile flat track in 1940 or 1941. The "pudding bowl" helmets of the era were almost useless against side blows. *Scholfield collection*

A scene from the 1940 or 1941 Costa Mesa, California, TT (forerunner of motocross). No. 44 rider's Sport Scout has the factory accessory racing saddle and the special "square" aluminum cylinder heads tried briefly before the advent of the 1940 streamlined cylinders and heads. In the middle of the crowd stands a uniformed soldier; though not yet at war, America was starting its defense buildup. *Scholfield collection*

This 1940 shot of Albert Wolfe of Northampton, Pennsylvania, shows the classic half-mile track sliding style of brake-less racers. The track was at Hatfield (nice name), Pennsylvania. His time trial result: 28.75 seconds; not bad. *Baer family collection*

By the 1940s, old 101s could be bought for a song, making them a popular racing choice. But 101s didn't have enough ground clearance to suit some riders' styles. Could this rider have dragged the frame? *Baer family collection*

1942 Sport Scout Highlights

Only a few 1942 models were produced and no sales catalogs were published. All the 1942 non-military models were built prior to February 9, 1942, when the federal government forbade further production of civilian vehicles. Thirty-Fifty (and Four) production was terminated. Indian head tank emblems replaced the teardrop emblem, but some models may have had the teardrop emblem. Miscellaneous parts formerly chrome-plated were finished with enamel. Some 1941 motor and frame numbers were used on 1942 models built after October 3, when normally all models in production would be for the next season.

War Clouds

As the first 1942 models were being built in the closing months of 1941, even before the United States entered World War II, the U.S. economy was already dominated by war. Internal

This 1941 Sport Scout is finished in Kashan green and black, which would have been an extra-cost option because Kashan green was not a standard offering for 1941.

Left: This treasure—an original unrestored 1941 Sport Scout—has only 66 original miles! The bike was stored during World War II and its owner never returned. Included in the recent sales package was all the original Indian dealership paperwork—the time purchase contract, license receipt, and even the salesman's business card!

1941 documents at Harley-Davidson are revealing. Steel shipments to support identified military motorcycle production were four months late, and additional aluminum was unobtainable. Doubtless, Indian faced the same raw materials shortages. The American metals industry was maximizing profits by satisfying the high-paying governments of the Allied Powers, so significant production of 1942 civilian motorcycles was going to be impossible. Both companies faced the dilemma of restricted civilian motorcycle production but the possibility of huge military motorcycle orders. Both Indian and Harley-Davidson had pursued military motorcycle orders for three years, and they were ready to return their half-idle factories to production levels not seen since 1929 in order to fill military orders. The suspense was broken with the Japanese attack on Pearl Harbor, which brought the United States into the war.

Chapter Six

Inside the Indian Factory: An Eyewitness Account by Allen Carter:
1942–1945

Prior to America's entry into World War II, Indian built two basic military models that were intended to capture the bulk of the military orders. The Model 640B was basically a militarized 45-ci Sport Scout. The Model 741 was a 30.50-ci outgrowth of the civilian Thirty-fifty, but featuring a Sport Scout-style package of engine, primary drive, and transmission. Both machines were produced with minor variations such as changing styles of air cleaners and varying tank-top data plates.

Indian's primary World War II motorcycle was the Model 741. The "cheese grater" enclosure between the cylinders acted as a radio static depressor to minimize interference with nearby communications.

The general layout of the Model 741 frame and powerplant assembly followed Sport Scout practice, but the engine capacity of 30.50 ci continued the little twin tradition. Indian chose the smaller engine size in response to the military specifications of foreign governments, which asked for 30.50-ci (500-cc) engines because this was a common capacity everywhere but in the United States.
Baer family collection

Indian built Model 741 motorcycles in an aging factory, and was often forced to use sub-standard materials due to wartime shortages.
Baer family collection

The Model 741 was in response to worldwide governmental procurement practices, in which design requirements were laid out in descriptive specifications. Except for the United States, the predominant middleweight motorcycles of the world featured engines of 30.50 -ci. It would thus be easier for Indian to squeeze into these foreign armies—which were already at war—by producing a 30.50-ci military model than by producing a 45-ci model. Unfortunately for Indian, the American Army used Harley-Davidsons exclusively. Those Model 640B and 741 Indians that had been delivered, if any, were soon absorbed into the armies of the Allies. Total Indian war years sales were about 39,000, compared to Harley-Davidson's total of about 88,000. The war thus proved more beneficial to Harley-Davidson than to Indian. Harley-Davidson was able to efficiently operate as a motorcycle manufacturer throughout the conflict, while Indian suffered the inefficiencies of infusing lots of non-motorcycle work into their factory product.

The Wigwam

Carter recalls:

I went up there (to Indian) in 1940, and stayed there until 1945. We were the end of it (big time motorcycle production). The motorcycle industry heyday (was) back before automobiles (were popular), when roads were bad and you could ride along the edge of the road on your motorcycle. After that it dropped down to nothing but police work.

It (the factory) was a flatiron (triangular) building. Wilbraham Road was on one side and the Boston Post Road (State Street) was on the other. It was an old-type factory. When you went in the front door, the stairway was there, built along the partitions. There was a big wide pair of steps that went up to the second floor. On the left side you went through doors and went right out in the factory. And on the right (first floor) was the receptionist, and the rest of the room was the sales manager and all their offices.

On the first floor was the sales office, and the comptroller was there. You walked through the main door and turned right. They had a receptionist there, and there were lots of old motorcycles around in this reception thing. The factory was beautifully done. It was done up like a museum—beautiful. All the offices on that first floor in that section were beautifully done, with oak paneling, like they did things back in those days. And then on the second floor was an engineering department. The design engineers had an office there. And on the third floor we had blueprint rooms, drawing storage, factory control stuff . . . Off of that was the experimental department. We had a machine shop, and we had a dynamometer room to test engines.

On the second floor there was a landing, and you went into there (to the offices), and that's where Briggs Weaver was, and Bob Powell. That went on up to the third floor where we had the blueprint room, and we had some detail draftsmen up there that detailed various things. Off of that, in the back of it, we had the experimental room—the machine shop. From then on it went over to the dynamometer room and on down the side of the building where we made the experimental frames

Allen Carter

In 1925, while in his 20s, Allen Carter went to work as an apprentice for DuPont Motors in Wilmington, Delaware. E. Paul du Pont was manufacturing the luxurious DuPont automobile, a car comparable to the better known Dusenberg. Carter was designated a riding mechanic for the DuPont Motors racing team sent to the Le Mans 24-hour race in France in the late 1920s.

When production of DuPont automobiles ceased in 1930, he was retained as the service manager in order to honor warranties. Carter performed this work while gradually assuming other duties for Mr. du Pont and the du Pont family. In the 1960s, Rolls-Royce authorized a unique arrangement, designating Carter's facility as an official Rolls-Royce service center. It was the only non-dealer Rolls maintenance facility in the world. Carter owned and operated the Wilmington Harley-Davidson dealership for a number of years. Meanwhile, on paper, DuPont Motors continued to exist into the 1990s. Although no one ever put this to the test, over 60 years after the last DuPont automobile was built, it would have been possible to have a DuPont car serviced in the same building where it had been launched, and by Allen Carter, who was the same mechanic who had prepped the car when new! Carter road-tested Indians at the Du Pont estate in Wilmington during the 1930s. His official Indian involvement was during the World War II years, when the factory needed him to help with the pressures of military contracts.

Indian built approximately 39,000 military bikes during World War II, the great bulk of which were Model 741 motorcycles. Harley built almost three times as many motorcycles as Indian during the war.

and things of that nature. (The fourth floor) was just storage up there. That's where we had all the old hillclimb machines and everything else.

Briggs Weaver was doing all the designing: in fact, he designed the Sport Scout. All the old people were gone. The only one there who had been there before as a test engineer was Jim Taylor. I went up there primarily as just a test engineer. We built an aero cycle for the paratroopers, and I had a lot to do with that, not designing, but putting it together and getting it made. I had a room set up about as big as this restaurant (30 feet by 60 feet), and I did a lot of work in there. In fact, I fooled around with the four-cylinder engine. Jim (Hill) and I worked together. When we got the order for the 841s, Jim had charge of the production of all that. He set up a shop within the factory, and Jim took care or all that. He ran that whole thing.

We had Frenchy Castonguay and Woodsie (Castonguay); they were test riders during the war. And we had Art Tramontin; he was a test rider. We all did a lot of riding and a lot of testing.

Indian's Non-riding Managers!

Carter tells us about motorcycle executives who wouldn't ride motorcycles:

The big problem was that we had people doing things that didn't have the basic experience with motorcycles, where Harley did, because young Bill Harley and the [Davidson] guys, they grew up with motorcycles. It [Harley-Davidson] was a family takeover. Well, this [Indian] was different.

We didn't have [riding executives] up there. I remember one time, we were building the aero cycle for the paratroopers, that lightweight cycle which was a helluva good little motorcycle. One day I was out in front of the place, and Briggs Weaver came along. It was cold weather. "Briggs," I said, "stay here with the motorcycle for a minute while I go inside and get my rain suit on. "Not thinking, I got off—I was sitting on it—I got off of it before I put the kickstand down, and I handed him the handlebars, to Briggs. He let go, and the motorcycle fell over. He wouldn't even hold the thing up; he didn't know what to do. The thing fell over, and I had to pick it up and put it on the side-stand. We had never had anyone there that really knew what the requirements were to build a good motorcycle.

We had guys up in the engineering department who had never ridden a motorcycle in their life. Briggs [Weaver] never [rarely] rode a motorcycle. Joe Hosley [plant manager], the gentleman, he had never ridden a motorcycle. Mr. du Pont had. All of the guys, the lesser engineers that did the detailed work and stuff like that, none of them had ever ridden a motorcycle. Walt Brown, myself, and Jimmy Hill, and Pop Armstrong, we were all motorcyclists. And we couldn't get these guys to do things. That was one of the problems, the fact that we had people in positions that didn't know anything about a motorcycle. It was kind of sad.

Bob Powell, now, the young guy that came in with Briggs later, he [rode]. Bob designed most of the aero cycle, and that worked real well. That we built for the paratroopers, but we never got production; the war was over. We only built a couple of them, experimentally. But we had an order, but the war ended before we got into production. Bob did most of the work on that. That was real good. The handlebars were in the right place and the seat was in the right place, because he rode a motorcycle.

Jim Hill, Walt Brown, Pop Armstrong, and myself would all get together once in awhile and try to gang up on the guys in the engineering department, to do this or do that. Of course, they thought we were a bunch of roughnecks.

Right in the middle of everything, Joe Hosley died. Then he [President du Pont] took in Moody and made him general manger. Moody, before that, had only been a purchasing agent in the company. He was a nice guy but he had no practical experience in motorcycles. But the whole Harley-Davidson outfit, both of those families were involved in the thing and they had somebody to come along all the time [being groomed for management], that really knew what the hell the score was. We never had that at all, so we wound up with a lot of people in jobs that really didn't know motorcycles.

The Worn-Out Factory

Indian's on-again-off-again production runs were doubly costly because of their worn-out production equipment and make-do methods. Carter reminiscences:

Indian, at one time, when old (George) Hendee had the thing, they were the leaders. And they had put all that new machinery in that place up at Wilbraham Avenue in Springfield, and that plant was new. But years ago (before World War II) everything got worn out in there. It was an old worn-out plant when Mr. du Pont took it over during the Depression. Nothing got replaced. When we were struggling, when I was up there during the war, we were still struggling with some of those old turret lathes and stuff that Hendee had bought. We had a whole damn big factory full of old worn-out machines. We couldn't hold the tolerances; we just didn't have the machines that would do it.

If they had a milling machine set up, that milling machine had enough tools to make maybe five parts. They would build maybe a hundred motorcycles at a shot. So the guy down there, the machine operator, he would get an order and a number for a certain piece that he was going to make. He would go down behind the machine and pick up these jigs and things and put them on the machine, and clamp them on, to make that part. That one machine might make five or six different parts, by adding and taking away different fixtures from it. And the whole plant was that way.

So, to change something, a minor change, would be disastrous. Because you would have to go down, and find out where that was going to be made at, what machine in the plant—it was a big plant, four stories high—you had to find the machine. And then the toolmakers would come along and check it to see what change they had to make in these fixtures to make the change on the part. The whole thing would take maybe two weeks before you could get this change made for production, or sometimes even longer.

So those were a lot of the problems. All we had were old profilers, milling machines, all kinds of automatic screw machines, and everything, but there wasn't one machine in there that could make (just) one part. We didn't have the production (to set up for single part operations). Every machine in there made more than one part. Well, not every one, but most of them. You had to set them up and break them down, set them up and break them down . . . You would have one machine operator, and he would be in a place maybe as big as this room (20

Indian built a few examples of the Model 640B, a military version of the Sport Scout. The U.S. Army preferred the Indian left-hand throttle because it facilitated right-hand transfer of messages between the rider and other vehicles, but testers favored Harley fenders for their additional tire clearance. A distinguishing characteristic of the Model 640B was the thick-wall cast-aluminum air intake pipe.

The Army wanted a shaft-drive bike for desert warfare, not for the European scene depicted here. In May of 1943 the Germans surrendered in North Africa, and in July the Army cancelled plans for mass-scale production of both the Indian Model 841 and the rival Harley-Davidson Model XA shaft drive. Our rider is Robin Markey.

Indian originally designed the Model 841 engine for an aircraft or ship standby generator, so they had an ideal engine on hand when the U.S. Army requested the design of a shaft-drive bike. Indian also had previously designed the frame as part of its projected postwar program. Indian and Harley-Davidson each built 1,000 shaft-drive bikes for evaluation, the Harley bike being basically a copy of the German Army BMW.

feet by 30 feet), and he would have three or four machines sitting around in there . . . You would come down and issue a work order, and he would see where the change was to be made. He would get it (the work order) and the production people would bring up the raw materials. And then he would set up the machines to make the thing. Then, after he got started, he would have to check it to see if it was to the right tolerances, and all like that. It took weeks, sometimes, to get the simplest thing through that plant.

Poor Materials

Carter Recalls How Poor Materials Plagued Indian:

We had a terrible time up there (at Indian). One of the worst things was . . . —we didn't have a good enough standing that we could use virgin material. People would turn in pots and pans, and we used all this secondary aluminum, like pistons.

God almighty! We had a terrible time getting through that. Our cylinder heads on a 74 for the Army—we were building those to go to Russia, 74s with sidecars—and part of the specifications was, it had to maintain 55 miles an hour with a 500-pound-weight in the sidecar. Boy, that was a job! We couldn't do that, because what would happen, these cylinder heads were made out of secondary aluminum, and we would blow holes and the spark plugs would come right out of that thing. They would get so damned hot that they would burn a hole right at the spark plug, and it blew the plug out and you would have a hole in the cylinder head (as big as a 50-cent piece). The pistons, we had to allow, oh, about a thousandths more on the piston clearance than you would on a regular piston. So we had ring problems. We had oil problems. We had lots of problems.

Harley-Davidson Helped Indian!

Strange as it may seem, Harley-Davidson sometimes helped its rival. Carter relates:

Harley and Indian really got along pretty well together, because Harley really wanted Indian to succeed. It would've been much better if there were two companies, because the interest was there and everything else. Harley did everything in the world to keep Indian alive.

I remember, during the war, we couldn't get the ignition switches any longer. So, Harley said, well, use ours. You've seen some of the military (switches); they're the same (on Harleys and Indians) . . . They had developed that switch years and years ago.

And it was the same way with the buddy seat. We wanted to have a buddy seat. Harley had a patent on that, the springs that come up, and whatnot. So, we tried to get around that every way we could. Finally, Harley knew we were doing it, and said, oh hell, go ahead and build them. Harley was very good. It was to its advantage to have Indian stay in business.

Harley was very helpful. In fact, experimentally, when we, during the war, were changing over to the hydraulic tappets, well Harley already had them. We were trying to develop the engines with the hydraulic tappets. We were having terrible trouble. One thing was, our oil pumps weren't large enough, didn't have enough pressure to recharge the hydraulic tappet. So Harley helped us out on that; they said you've got to change the pump, this, that and the other; you're going to need 25 pounds of pressure, pretty much even at idle, or otherwise the tappet would leak down. So they were helpful; they really were.

No Pliers, No Motorcycles

When the government bought motorcycles, they were extremely specific as to what they were to be delivered. A complete military motorcycle included the complete toolkit as defined in the contract, and the complete toolkit included every single item listed in the contract. Every item.

It so happened that Indian ran out of valve cover pliers. This was a minor annoyance at first, but the matter became alarming when otherwise complete motorcycles were parked in the storage

99

This was Indian's first foot-shift bike and featured a right-hand clutch lever in conjunction with the traditional left-hand throttle. Power was transmitted through a primary drive chain to a four-speed "crash" box (not a constant mesh).

building. Row upon row of olive drab Indians sat there gathering dust because the government would not accept delivery of the bikes without the complete tool kit. No valve cover pliers meant no motorcycle deliveries, and no deliveries meant no progress payments. Indian was in effect loaning money interest-free to the government!

Carter takes up the story:

The valve covers on the Indian (are) knurled (and require special pliers). Well, (the pliers) got too expensive to make during the war, and we couldn't get them anymore. Every one of those had to go in the toolbox of an army machine. We were in a terrible fix; we can't produce any machines. We sent an order down to the tool-making department, and they were going to make some (manufacturing) tools up to make this thing. In the meantime, we're way behind in production. In fact, they sent somebody up from Springfield Ordnance to see whether we were sabotaging the effort, because we weren't sending any motorcycles. So I thought, why hell, we got a problem. None of those guys in there had ever seen a pair of water pump pliers. Anyway, I went down to an old automobile parts house in Springfield. I bought a pair of them and I came back. By cutting the handles off a little short, they would fit in the toolbox. We found out the tool company that

made them was up in Buffalo, New York. So we called them up and they said hell yeah, they could supply some. So we said, "can you cut them off 2-1/2 inches?" They said, "Sure, no problem at all; we got barrels of them." The war was on, and they couldn't sell them. These worked fine; you take those valve covers, and you could take them down fine.

Things of that nature, we were just up against it. The main thing was, the setup was made years and years ago, when Hendee had it. We could never, never—we didn't have the orders in the first place—we could never produce like Harley-Davidson could. They were in a better location, for one thing. They could buy tools and machines from automobile factories that were changing over. Harley could buy a lot of stuff better than what we could ever do, because they were in a better location.

The Shaft-Drive Army Twin, Model 841

Both Indian and Harley-Davidson built 1,000 shaft-drive motorcycles for the Army during World War II. Harley's effort was a copy of the German BMW but Indian's shaft-drive bike was an all-new design. Indian's inquisitive president E. Paul du Pont instigated the effort by modifying his Morgan three-wheeled car, as Carter relates:

It was his [Paul du Pont's] idea to build the 90-degree motorcycles. He rode a motorcycle and he knew how bad it vibrated and whatnot, and it was his idea to build a motorcycle to be free of vibration. In the old engine you had two choices. You could balance it so the vibration would be up and down or so it would be back and forth. So the trick was to try to have a happy medium, and get it to have just a little bit of back and forth because the motorcycle would (absorb it). Years ago down at the shop, when a motorcycle took off—we had a cinder road—you could see a cinder pattern where the cylinders had fired. Of course, when they put the shock hub on the engine that helped a lot.

Indian's hands-on president E. Paul du Pont designed the crankcase for a 90-degree V-twin prototype engine! Carter recalls:

They sent the [prototype] engine down and I was the one who put it in a frame. That was a 74-ci (90-degree twin). They had built an ammunition carrier for the Army, a three-wheeled "Dispatch Tow," only it had a military box on the back. That had a 74 engine in it. It was down in Aberdeen (Aberdeen Proving Grounds, Maryland), so I went down and got it, and brought it up from Aberdeen, took the engine out, and then went ahead and put this 90-degree engine in there.

Postwar Plans

Parallel Plots

Postwar planning envisioned an end to the historic Indian lineup. The three distinct types—the Chief, the Sport Scout, and the Four— had very few parts in common, these being mainly bits and pieces such as bolts, nuts, screws, clips, and so forth. E. Paul du Pont chartered the engineering department to develop a lineup of motorcycles that would share such major components as cylinders, cylinder heads, pistons, connecting rods, valves, and so on. Substantial production savings could be realized from this modular approach.

An inline four-cylinder "X-44" motorcycle was completed. In fact, the frame of the X-44 was used for the army Model 841. The frame was influenced by BMW practice, and the engine by the twin high-camshaft designs of the Riley automobile and Triumph motorcycle, both of which, incidentally, had been designed by Triumph's Edward Turner. The modular lineup was to be completed by creation of a lightweight single-cylinder motorcycle and a middleweight twin. To achieve maximum commonality the twin would have used a side-by-side cylinder layout, the fabled "vertical" twin popularized by Triumph. This would have permitted the same tooling to be used to finish the crankcases of the four, the twin, and the single, since all center-to-center distances would have been the same.

Designer G. Briggs Weaver left Indian during the war, taking with him the modular motorcycle concept. In 1944, Weaver designed his own family of modular bikes for the Torque Engineering Company of Plainfield, Connecticut. Although Weaver's inline four-cylinder never went into production, his single-cylinder lightweight and vertical twin-cylinder middleweights were produced as the 1949 Indian Arrow and Indian Scout.

The only way I could do it—Mr. du Pont had an English Morgan that had the engine in it. I could take it. Then we had an engine, but we had no way to start it, no transmission, nothing, just an engine. All it had was a little shaft sticking out the back. So I found out that the flywheel off the Morgan, if I took it and put it on the Indian engine in the frame, I would have a starter and a clutch. Then I had no transmission, so I took the transmission out of the Morgan, which was shaft drive back to the gearbox and was chain drive from the gearbox back to the rear wheel. The Morgan had only one rear wheel; now we had two. The back axle on this was from a Model T Ford, with a hole cut through for the chain drive of the regular Indian engine. So I had to shift the back wheels over about an inch to line it up with the transmission, which I did. When you saw it, you wouldn't notice it. It had an electric starter and it worked real good.

Frank Long (Indian's Washington, D. C. Army coordinator) brought these guys up, these two Army guys—I think one was a colonel. They were in the transportation department, and they rode the thing down at the old DuPont Motors plant. They rode it all around; that was where they got the idea to give us an order for a thousand of them. In order to do that, they had to give Harley-Davidson something. Harley-Davidson didn't have anything in the works, no designs or anything, so they just copied a BMW, which was the thing to do. But in the meantime we had gone ahead and designed the motorcycle with a 45-ci engine in the thing.

Indian made two of the 74-ci tricycles. The smaller one was the one that I put the 90-degree engine in. And they made another one that was larger. It had a wider rear end on it and it had a larger box on it. It was down at Aberdeen. They tested that at Aberdeen and we had problems with it. I think Harley got a contract to build some of them (trikes) but Indian didn't. It was there for a long time. I went down and brought it back. I kept it in Wilmington for four or five months. Then one day they wanted it back up in Springfield, and I drove it up there. It was an ammunition carrier and was made to haul 500 pounds.

The (841) engine was built in Springfield and tested in Wilmington. They (the factory) were too busy. They had an order for the French government for 5,000 74s with sidecars, and they (the factory) didn't have time to do anything.

There were visions of a military bonanza for Indian. Movie theaters showed newsreels every week, and the public was accustomed to seeing clips of German army action, and where there was German army action there were German army motorcycles. Lots of them. Motorcycles had been an important element in the German army's lightning "blitzkrieg" warfare. For Indian, it seemed their shaft-drive transverse V-twin Model 841 was a sure winner, for the bike was similar in concept to the German BMW shaft-drive twins. Harley-Davidson management was also starry-eyed. But they knew how to save a buck in Milwaukee; instead of designing something akin to the German bike, they simply copied it! We know now that the American Army Jeep became the dominant mobile force for general military transportation.

Carter recalls how the 841 project came to a halt:

They (the Army) went out to El Centro, California, before we invaded North Africa. They assembled all this stuff they were going to use in North Africa out at El Centro. So we sent Walt Brown out there. Walt Brown was a great big guy, and he was a test engineer. They got out there in the desert, and, of course, Willys was there with a Jeep. Now there's no question. You couldn't ride a motorcycle in sand 6 inches deep. Walt was out there for about three or four months and he couldn't do anything with the motorcycle. The minute they got off any kind of built-up road they were stuck because you cannot ride a motorcycle in deep sand. At that time they were just bringing out tubeless tires made of synthetic rubber. But with spoked wheels we couldn't go to tubeless tires. We tried, with all kinds of sealers around and everything else. The Jeep was the end of the motorcycle. Of course we got some orders; they wanted them for messengers and stuff like that, but not in the quantities that (we had hoped).

The Jeep killed off all big-time motorcycle possibilities, not just those of the Model 841. During the U.S. participation in World War II, Indian built a total of 39,054 motorcycles, all military models except for a few hundred police bikes. Although Harley-Davidson built about double

this number, both companies' outputs were tiny in relation to Jeep production of over 639,000 units. Yet Harley-Davidson's production was sufficient to keep it efficiently operating at what it did best: building motorcycles. Indian, in contrast, found itself ramping up and down on small motorcycle contracts, and switching in and out of small production runs on non-motorcycle items like landing gear components.

Another Job for the 841 Engine

Although the Model 841 motorcycle didn't have a big future, there remained other possibilities for the 841 powerplant. The military used Scout-sized engines for lots of jobs such as standby aircraft generators, aircraft ground support (maintenance) generators, and power wenches. Carter remembers how Indian pursued an opportunity to use the 841 as a generator for blimps. The work was done under a "development" contract, which meant that large production and significant profits hinged on passing the test program. Working closely with Indian was the Lawrence Aeronautical Corporation, which had merged with Indian.

Carter recalls:

Melvin Rhoades came up with them from Lawrence [Lawrence Aeronautical Corp.] and they made a botch of the thing. They really did. It (the Lawrence engine) was a five-cylinder radial engine. It was to drive a 7-1/2 KW generator. It would take about 30 horsepower. We took the 841 engine, and put a shroud around it, and a blower on it. The generator and everything had to weigh 325 pounds. We went down to the center in Fort Monmouth, New Jersey, where stuff was being tested for the Army. You could get 30 horsepower out of it. It was running pretty well wide open. It had to run 150 hours for a test. It would do a 150 hours, but at the end of the 150 hours the engine was junk. That's a long time. That was pretty close to the limit of what that engine would produce. We passed the test, except we were about 50 pounds overweight. Then the war ended.

How a Crushing Bureaucracy Costs Millions at War's End

"One of the worst downfalls we had was when the war was pretty much over and Joe Hosley died," Carter reminisces:

Moody was the general manager. We used to have a guy named Doug Overbaugh. He had these big huge ledger books up in a special room. And he had one woman that worked for him, for years. That's where he generated the orders to make the

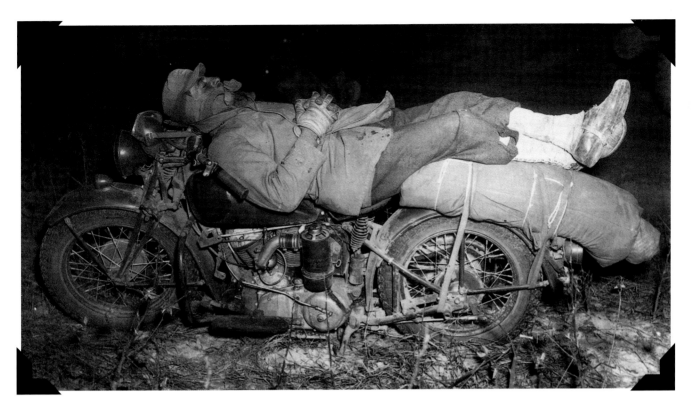

parts in the factory. He had these huge ledger books; there must've been 8 or 10 of them, great big thick things with big sheets. He would open those up, and he could tell you where a certain part was in the plant, how many operations were on it. He always knew that. He watched, and he could tell by the cards the men turned in at nighttime, where the part was, how many operations were on; he could tell you the whole thing.

Well, somebody got the idea that was old fashioned, and that they should bring in IBM, and do this thing with an IBM setup. That was what really was the downfall of the company. Because they came in, and the first thing they did, they said, "Well, all these tools that you have spread around these machines, with numbers on them to make certain parts, they ought to be in one place. When a guy gets an order to make something, he will call up someplace else and they'll bring up the tools for the machine." So they got rid of this (system) of Doug Overbaugh's that had worked for years and years just perfectly.

I could go down to Doug Overbaugh and say, Doug, "Where is so and so?" and he would say, "Well, just a minute. It's down in department 29, and he says right now it's got one more operation on it to finish it, or two, or three." That was great. You could do this in five minutes. He was on the second floor, down from where we were. And we'd go down there, and he could tell you right away. And if he wasn't there, there was a woman who worked for him.

Well, once the IBM thing came in, they decided to take all these tools all over the plant, all these special fixtures, and everything, and put them down in the cellar. And then they would issue the order to the guy in the cellar and he would pull the tools out to put on the different machines. Well, someplace along the line they didn't number these things right and they didn't fill the IBM cards out right, so they didn't know where in the hell they were. They had a whole cellar-full, tons and tons of jigs and fixtures. Some of it they could figure out but the rest of it they couldn't. So when the war was over, we had about seven Army contracts for various things. We were making parts for Boeing Aircraft and whatnot like that. We were working for, what was it, 10 percent? Ten percent over cost, or something like that. We couldn't justify where we were on the cost of all these pieces in the plant. So they [the government] wouldn't pay us.

I don't remember how many dollars were involved, but it was a helluva lot of money that we could never justify because we couldn't show our cost sheets on it. This whole thing was lost. They couldn't justify to the government for them to pay us for so many operations on a part. We were making stuff for Boeing Aircraft. We were making stuff for Springfield Arsenal. It wasn't all motorcycles; we were making shellings (casings) for 88-millimeter shells for explosion on contact. I think Indian got about one-third of the money that was due them. If they had left everything alone, they would've been all right.

An exhausted rider used his Model 640B as a bed. It's a good bet that this photo dates from America's 1940–1941 war preparedness period, because the U.S. Army bought only a handful of Model 640B bikes after testing these against Harley-Davidson WLA machines. Yeah, most likely a cold night in Louisiana. *Robin Markey collection*

103

Chapter Seven

New Bikes, Old Name, Last Glory:
1946–1953

A complex chain of events transformed the Indian Motorcycle Company in the immediate postwar years. Under E. Paul du Pont's presidency since 1930, Indian had been profitable only about half the time, and in the unprofitable years the losses were usually more than the profits in the good years. Du Pont decided to extricate himself from Indian, first with an offer to the Lawrence Aeronautical group. When this didn't pan out, du Pont sold Indian to a financial group headed by young industrialist Ralph B. Rogers in November 1945.

The Indian vertical twins lineup started out with the 440-cc 1949 Scouts and continued with the 500-cc 1950 and 1951 Warriors. This is a 1951 model. When the British devalued their currency in late 1948, this lowered the prices of comparable Brit bikes 30 percent overnight. The suddenly high-priced verticals were doomed.

Rogers, who had already turned around the struggling Cummins diesel engine company, was a certified whiz kid entrepreneur. Former Indian staffer Matt Keevers recalls, "Ralph Rogers could sell iceboxes to Eskimos." Rogers had a new vision for Indian. Impressed by the modern lightweight motorcycles he observed on a European tour, he was convinced that if the old Indian name were coupled with truly new motorcycles, Indian could break away from the old self-limited market and recruit many thousands of newcomers into motorcycling. How many thousands? Over 100,000 new Indians could be sold per year, Rogers suggested, in light of the current six-figure sales of motorbikes and motor scooters. In a way, Rogers was going back to the "better mousetrap" theory that had been the foundation of the original Scout back in 1920. But Rogers would add to the stew a modern advertising campaign relying on extensive celebrity endorsements. (Rogers' Indian promotional plan was strikingly similar to the later famous Honda campaign: "You meet the nicest people on a Honda.")

Rogers' strategy for Indian was no less than a revolution. Time would either be an ally or an enemy, so Rogers saved as much time as he could. He started with a strong and famous dealer network, and he soon bought the Torque Manufacturing Company of Plainfield, Connecticut. During the war, the Torque company had employed G. Briggs Weaver, former Indian chief engineer, to design a line of modular motorcycles. So Rogers had in hand the designs and the prototypes of lightweight motorcycles of advanced specifications. Consequently, Rogers avoided two major time consumers: building a dealer network and designing a product line. The single-cylinder "Torque Model" went into engineering testing in March 1946.

The Rogers master plan didn't include the traditional big Indians, the Chief, the Sport Scout, and the Four. But he needed to keep the dealers in business under the Indian banner, so the money-making Chief was continued as the sole 1946 Indian model. For the first time since the 1920 season, there was no middleweight Indian bearing the name Scout.

Proposed 1947 Sport Scout

In the meantime, Rogers allowed engineering planning to continue on a proposed 1947 Sport Scout. An April 26, 1946, report to the Board of

Directors cited 18 improvements over the last production Sport Scouts of 1942, and these are quoted as follows:

1. New-type gear feed pump with new larger crankcases.
2. Rear generator drive similar to Model 346.
3. Model 346 front fork, handlebar, and wheel assembly.
4. Modified rear spring frame, using springs arrangement similar to Model 346.
5. Rear wheel brake plate assembly similar to Model 346.
6. Improved saddle springing with new saddle bracket.
7. Improved side prop stand.
8. Center stand modified, using Model 346 features.
9. New rear hollow axle assembly.
10. New fork valve lifter.
11. Redesigned cams, to eliminate manufacturing problems.
12. New muffler and tailpipe assembly, similar to Model 346.
13. New chain guard, incorporating Model 346 improvements.
14. New rear brake drum, similar to Model 346.
15. Seam-welded gasoline tanks, using Model 841 stampings.
16. Steel-forged flywheels.
17. Steel inserts installed in front and rear cylinders at intake ports to eliminate strip ping of threads at assembly.
18. New-type valve covers, same as Model 346.

The June 28, 1946, Report to the Board of Directors discussed engineering progress on the Proposed Model 647 Sport Scout:

Engineering is well into its program for the changes on Model 647 motorcycle and in the order of improved features listed in the last report to the Board of Directors, Engineering has completed items 1, 3, 4, 5, 9, 10, 13, 14, 15, and 16. There remain yet to be completed items 2, 6, 7, 8, 11, 12, and 17.

With reference to item 18, new-type valve covers will not be required on the proposed Model

Shortly after World War II, many war surplus Model 741 Indians were bought by transportation-starved Europeans who then demilitarized the bikes. Consequently, decades later the Model 741 remains prominent in the European Indian movement. This "civilianized" Dutch example typifies this important category of Indians that have evolved from everyday riders to collectibles.

Some postwar riders gave their Sport Scouts the popular "bobber" treatment, the term referring to cut-off or "bobbed" fenders. Some rode with a bobbed front fender, others liked the naked front tire for its racy look. Another bobber hallmark was custom high-riser handlebars. Bobbers started in the 1920s and were always popular in California. Some riders did indeed use a World War II aircraft mascot in the decor. This bobber, owned by *Cycle World* magazine editor David Edwards, was part of the Guggenheim's *Art of the Motorcycle* exhibit. *Brian Blades*/Cycle World

647, due to the fact that other changes require revision of the cylinder casting and the valve compartment being incorporated in the cylinder casting, eliminating necessity of separate valve covers.

It has been decided that one of the major features on the Model 647 will be the incorporation of the foot gearshift and hand clutch. The engineering of these features is well along. With the present engineering forces it will be August before the

Engineering Department can complete all of their work on these revised designs, because of the above major design changes.

Despite the effort on the proposed Model 647 Sport Scout, the June 28, 1946, report stated:

> The Model 647 is scheduled for production this fall. It would appear from present conditions that materials, plant capacity, etc., will make this impossible. However, the Model 647 will be on the market at the earliest possible date.

In August 1946 a Monday morning press release mentioned the Model 647 Sport Scout was under way. From the September 19, 1946, Report to the Board of Directors:

> Engineering is substantially completed on the Model 647 motorcycle . . . We are proceeding as rapidly as possible to put the Model 647 in production. It is certain at this time that next spring will be the very earliest date for its production . . .

The Model 647 was never again mentioned in internal company documents.

A headline in the *Springfield Daily News* of October 16, 1947, read: "Motorcycle at Lower Price Planned by Indian Company; Will Make Radically-New Product at East Springfield Plant Starting Next Spring." Meanwhile, for the 1947 season, Indian continued to offer only the Chief.

1946 and 1947 Racing

Postwar racing didn't explode on the scene and instantly reach the level of prewar activity. There was no 1946 Daytona 200, for example.

Immediately after the war, Ed Kretz Sr. resumed the dominance of TT racing that had been his since the mid-1930s. TT racing permitted brakes, but in this case Kretz used the rear brake only. The tougher the course, the better "the Iron Man" did. *Kretz family collection*

Indian moved the Edison Splitdorf magneto directly onto the oil pump. This eliminated the ambiguity or "slop" in the former magneto drive system (which was taken off the rear of the primary chain). The factory used surplus Model 741 frames on the Model 648. These differ in several ways from the Sport Scout rigid frame of 1934–1939, most notably in the lack of a vertical brace on the rear section.

Meanwhile, Indian had farmed out its prewar Big Base Scouts. Jack Armstrong (son of Pop Armstrong) relates:

> After the war was over, they gave Spieglehoff one, they gave Edwards one, they gave Kretz one, and one had disappeared. Nobody knows who got it, where it would have went. There's speculation, but there were never any fingers pointed. I think—I don't know—but I think Kretz turned his back in again. He may have thought, and maybe rightfully so, that he could build an engine out there in California that would be as good as the prewar Big Base Scout engine.

In 1946, the classic Laconia 100-mile road race fell to Indian's Ed Kretz, and the Langhorne 100-mile speedway (long, steeply banked track) fell to Indian's Johnny Spiegelhoff. Harley's Jimmy Chann won the Springfield 25-mile

The Model 648 Daytona Scout racer was an outgrowth of racing development begun in 1941. These are popularly termed "Big Base" Scouts because of larger crankcase volume. The fork is the same used on the Model 741; it's about 1 inch longer and provided extra ground clearance for "crossed up" sideways sliding on dirt tracks.

Indian revived the time-honored Scout name for the 1949 26.6-ci (440-cc) vertical twin. A fully serviced weight of only about 315 pounds produced competitive acceleration with the flood of British 30.50-ci motorcycles. The concept of a lightweight medium-sized motorcycle remains attractive today. But Indian's execution of the concept was flawed by various technical problems, chiefly difficult starting caused by a faulty magneto.

The Scout and companion single-cylinder Arrow were the first American-designed foot-shift motorcycles for the buying public. But the bikes weren't created by Indian; Indian bought the design rights from the Torque Manufacturing Company. Three variants were offered: a basic "Scout," a "Sport Scout," and a "Super Scout."

national on the one-mile track, thus breaking Indian's stranglehold. For some years, the Springfield winner had been rewarded with the honor of carrying the No. 1 plate until the next Springfield national, so Harley-Davidson advertisements would enjoy this aspect. Milwaukee also had a handle on their racing future—they built 100 racing WR models in 1946.

Planning the Postwar Model 648

From Jack Armstrong, we learn of Indian's progress in designing the Model 648:

At the end of 1946, Indian started to play with the idea of possibly utilizing some of the pieces and parts that they had left over from the war. Some people had tried the 841 flywheels, prior to 1948, and were successful in using them. We knew that the 841 cylinders were better, because they were cast by Brown and Sharpe, and they had the heavy (so-called "square") bases on them. That was one of the things with Indian: if you weren't too careful it would pop a front cylinder off. Well, with these Brown and Sharpe cylinders, where they were heavier around the base, they wouldn't blow off as quick.

So by the time 1947 rolled around, Indian knew (what to do), and when I say "Indian" knew,

I'm not talking the president or vice president or anything like that. I'm talking Jimmy Hill, Willard Wolfe, Pop Armstrong, and Walt Brown. They took one of the bases, and they sent it out, and I don't know what the casting company was. It was local, in Connecticut somewhere, I think. And they copied that one Big Base. And this prewar Big Base, (with) 841 flywheels, standard Sport Scout connecting rods, . . . the 841 cylinders, . . . and the large fin heads . . . had been (available) since (late) 1939. I think the (piston) company was Judson. A two-ring piston, a two compression ring piston. They used the 640 crank. They used the 741 forks from the war, and the 741 wheels. This was the combination that they used to base their new Big Base engine on.

Meanwhile, Indian's 1947 racing season got off to a great start at Daytona Beach. Jack Horn and Bull Hugeley won first and second places in the 100-mile national championship for the amateur class. (Incidentally, the "term" amateur was misleading because riders in this class were professionals.) The next day, Johnny Spiegelhoff rode one of the prewar, under-the-table Big Base Sport Scouts to victory in the Daytona 200 national

championship (expert class). But aside from the Daytona 200, Harley-Davidsons won the rest of the national championship races except the Langhorne 100-mile speedway national, which was taken by Norton rider Ed Guill.

To test the engine components of the hoped-for postwar racer, Jimmy Hill built up a racer for Jack Armstrong to ride in the 50-mile Novice Class Laconia road race. Armstrong relates:

In 1947, Jimmy Hill set me up with a 648 race bike that was exactly like the one they came out with in 1948, with the exception of the bases, the oil pump, the gas tank, and the fenders. Everything else was the same: the 841 wheels, the rods, the cylinders, the heads, Bonneville cams. And at that particular time there were three different Bonneville exhaust lifters—they had the short, medium, and long—and they used the long ones. Heavy. He set this up for me, him, and my Dad, so I could run the 50-miler (Novice Class). It was sort of a proving thing, to make sure that everything (on the forthcoming postwar Big Base jobs) was going to operate correctly. The truth is, I won the 50-miler (Novice class).

Here we see an unfinished Model 648 racer—the footboards have yet to be installed. The separate under-the-saddle oil tank, though counter to Indian tradition, had two advantages: the right fuel tank capacity was increased with the absence of an oil compartment, and there was no longer risk of fuel leaking into the oil compartment. *Matt Keevers collection*

Weighing in at about 260 pounds fully serviced, and with a hand clutch and foot shift, the 1949 Arrow had the potential to produce an explosive growth of new motorcyclists who otherwise were put off by heavy foot-clutch/hand-shift American motorcycles. But sales price was a big issue for first-time riders. Postwar inflation, quality control problems, and a horde of imported British bikes offered at fire-sale prices combined to price the Arrow out of the highly competitive small-motorcycle market.

As well as seeking more horsepower, the Indian staff was trying to improve reliability. Armstrong remembers:

> They were playing around with cam timing, too. They were trying to keep the same horsepower but produce it at 500 to 700 rpm slower engine speeds. Their approach was to lift the valves higher. This didn't work out. Part of the reason for this effort was the problem we had with Indian connecting rods. They used to break just below the wrist pin, which is worse than breaking on the lower end because when they break on the upper end they take out the whole engine. That's why Bill Tuman and the guys used to use Harley WR connecting rods. Even the drilled WR rods were stronger than the Indian rods.

Indian's aging crop of regular prewar Sport Scouts didn't share the under-the-table secrets of 1941 prototypes. Moreover, there weren't enough of them to meet postwar demand. Harley-Davidson built another 20 WR racers in 1947, and authorized production of yet another 292 WR racers to be built in the year ahead! In the 1947 Laconia 100, won by Harley-Davidson rider Alli Quattrochi, Indian's Ted Edwards finished second, but Harleys captured the rest of the top 10 places. The "insiders"—Jimmy Hill, Willard Wolfe, Pop Armstrong, and Walt Brown—had been planning all along to build a postwar racer. Thanks to the disappointing Laconia results, they were able to enlist the necessary financial support of the front office. The new racers would be designated the Model 648, but popularly termed "Big Base Scouts." The insiders hit the ground running; they didn't have to spend time figuring out what they wanted in the Model 648.

The 648 program produced a combination of complete motorcycles and uninstalled power-plants, totaling 50 units. The Model 648 had the big crankcases and gear-type oil pump pioneered just before the war, as well as Model 841 flywheels, and the longer fork of the Model 741 army bike.

Of the estimated 500 different parts used in the Model 648, only 10 were non-standard parts.

The Arrow was powered by a 13.3-ci (220-cc) single-cylinder overhead-valve engine. The "Silver Arrow" designation refers to the additional equipment of center stand, front safety guard, mirror, and luggage rack. A "Gold Arrow" substituted saddlebags for the luggage rack, and added twin spotlights and a windshield. The basic "Arrow" had none of these items.

This is an original unrestored 1950 Warrior. The major difference from the 1949 Scout was a larger engine capacity, 30.40 ci (500 cc). The twin-passenger seat was an Indian accessory. The bike also came equipped with a primary chain-tensioning device. Indian had claimed the 1949 primary drive didn't need one because the chain was pre-stretched!

Child's play for the great Indian factory? Not really. Of the standard parts, 65 were already on back-order to fill existing orders, and 420 parts were in stock. The estimated cost of the standard parts was $340 per motorcycle. The special parts situation was different. Here, the estimated cost was $365 per motorcycle. The 10 special parts cost more than the 490 standard parts!

The project moved rapidly ahead under the supervision of Jimmy Hill and Willard Wolfe. They had permission to use any factory resources in order to stay on schedule; they were even permitted to take any worker off the Chief final assembly line. Jack Armstrong recalls: "Each one of the full bikes that Indian sent out was first tested on the dyno for horsepower. And if they didn't meet the criterion that Jimmy and Willard set up, they would go back in, be torn back apart, and looked at to find out why." To get to the factory dynomometer, Hill recalls that he and Wolfe would ride the completed motorcycles through an upper-story covered bridge that connected the two main sections of the giant Wigwam. The barking exhaust pipes bounced the sound waves against the corrugated tin bridge enclosure in an unforgettable crescendo!

The net result was that Indian had to underwrite the cost—sell the motorcycles at a loss, in other words—to the tune of $400 per motorcycle.

The cost of the 648 program was trivial in comparison to the millions of dollars being spent on the Torque program. Under the banner of advertising, only a $20,000 net direct motorcycle cost was allotted to the program. Parallel to Indian's racing program of 25 motorcycles and 25 additional engines, Harley-Davidson was building 292 WR racers! The Indian racing "franchise" hadn't folded completely, but Sport Scouts were rapidly diminishing in the racing ranks, replaced either by Harleys or the increasing flood of British built bikes.

But there were more than the official 25-plus-25 units, in the opinion of Jack Armstrong.

They produced a lot of extra parts. That's why, today, people say that there's only a few of these Big Base motors left, the 648 type. That's not true, because there were parts and pieces made. I can remember my Dad telling me that when he was out traveling around the country, that the dealers wanted the factory to produce a 648 kit that they could put into a Scout. The factory didn't want to do it, because they didn't think it would be economically feasible. It certainly didn't pay when they made the Big Base jobs. They lost money on it; they knew that they were going to lose money. They were hoping that they were going to recoup the money in advertisement. But there were parts made, and that's why, today, I think if you can take a count, I

The 1950–1952 Warrior TT was tailored for off-road competition. Indian initially sold the bike stripped of lights and battery, but soon offered an electrical kit to make the bike street legal. To increase ground clearance to 7 inches, Indian made the fork 1-1/2 inches longer and fitted stiffer springs, and the rear section was raised by fitting a slipper bracket above each top coil spring and by fitting shorter bottom coil springs.

The saddle height was raised 1-1/2 inches by new mounting hardware. Other modifications included folding footpegs, an engine skid plate, a vented water-resistant magneto, a water-resisting check valve in the transmission (gearbox) breather, water-resistant pushrod seals, a variety of optional rear sprockets mounted by screws instead of rivets, 7.5:1 compression ratio (instead of 7:1), and a 3/8-inch rear chain (instead of 1/4 inch).

In the 1940s, Americans were infatuated by symmetry, thus automobile dashboards often included a clock that matched the size of the speedometer and was in the right-side mirror image position. Indian conformed to this thinking with the tank-top-mounted ignition switch that mimicked the fuel cap. According to Indian advertisements, in 1951 more nonprofessional TT races were won on Warrior TT bikes than on any other make and model.

think you'll find that there's more than just the allotted 50 Big Base motors around.

March 1948
Small Bet Pays Off at Daytona Beach

Floyd Emde won the 1948 Daytona 200 on a Model 648! His wire-to-wire lead in America's most prestigious race had cost the company a mere pittance of $20,000. This was about the amount of money invested in a single day of Chief production. Ralph Rogers stepped into the publicity photos, giving the appearance that his support was substantial instead of trivial. But the starting lineup of the Daytona 200 was evidence of the changing balance of power in American racing. Taking 1939 as a typical prewar year, the breakout of the 47 finishers showed Harley-Davidson at 48 percent, Indian at 36 percent, and all others at 16 percent. In 1948 the competing marques finishing were Harley-Davidson 51 percent, Indian 25 percent, and all others 25 percent. Except for a solitary BMW, "others" were English

motorcycles. Harley-Davidson was gaining; Indian was slipping.

1947–1948
The "Verticals" Move Toward Production

In early 1948, Rogers led a group of Indian executives on a national tour to introduce the new vertical twin Scouts and Arrow singles to Indian dealers. Rogers gave some of the details of the large financial investment being made in a new factory—the old Wigwam was to be abandoned—noting that over $6,600,000 had been spent, including a lot of his personal fortune. An advertising executive said, "The 200,000 guys on Whizzers and Servi-Cycles are really in training school for us." The briefing team spread optimism about Indian's future, and Rogers doubled the number of registered dealers from about 450 to about 900.

In the spring of 1948, Indian began relocating machinery and people from the Wigwam to a new East Springfield one-story plant. The new vertical twins and singles weren't ready in time for

Max Bubeck on his modified 1949 Scout vertical twin. The engine was enlarged to 30.50 ci and a more accurate speedometer was placed on the tank top. With the motorcycle in this configuration, Bubeck won California's prestigious Cactus Derby enduro. In such events, the rider was to maintain a predetermined average speed. Good enduro riders of the era had to be able to calculate averages in their head and to determine corrective speeds and times that would put them back on schedule. *Max Bubeck collection*

Ed Kretz Sr. jumps a 1949 Scout vertical twin in a California TT race. Note the huge rear sprocket. Kretz liked the power and handling of the vertical twins, but he soon switched to racing Triumphs, whose bikes and management were both more reliable than Indian's. *Kretz Family collection*

the all-important spring sales season, due largely to the same problems that had plagued Chief production-supplier-provided castings and heat treating. In May, Indian laid off 600 workers, drawing the factory roll down from 1,650 to 1,050. In the summer, when ordinarily production would start to ramp up on the next year's models, the decision was made not to offer a 1949-model Chief. This action was taken because of a number of production problems that plagued Arrow and Scout deliveries.

1948–1949 Disaster

Roughly 3,000 1948 Chiefs—one-fourth of the 1947 Chief production—kept Indian dealers in business while waiting for the promised Arrows and Scouts. In July 1948, the first Arrow singles were offered for sale from the company-owned store in Springfield. In August, the new East Springfield plant officially opened. The plant, however, wasn't automated to the degree that had been originally planned. Shortly after, both Arrows and vertical twin Scouts were being sold through-

out the nation. In choosing the "Scout" name for the twin, Indian was tying into the familiar and, hopefully, tying into the original magic. Could the new Scout excite and inspire dealers as had the original 1920 model? Would the new Arrow recruit "nice" people into motorcycling the way the 1920 Scout had excited them? The answers came soon. And forcefully.

The few Arrows and Scouts that were delivered proved very unreliable in the hands of riders. Crankcases filled up with oil when the motorcycles weren't ridden regularly. Dealers were advised to seat the oil check valve between the oil tank and the oil pump by using a hammer and punch on the valve! Engine tune-up specifications hadn't been thoroughly worked out before production. Following complaints about rough low-speed running, the factory sent out new settings for the spark plug gap, the magneto point gap, and the valve clearances.

Hard starting was the most common and most serious problem. The small magneto was adequate for the single-cylinder Arrow but inadequate

to handle the additional load of a distributor in the twin-cylinder Scout. According to factory road tester Jimmy Hill, the faulty magneto was a lower cost replacement for a preproduction unit that worked properly. The choke mechanism consisted of a slotted rotary disk fitted over the air cleaner element, and this setup sometimes leaked excessive air. Dealers were instructed to seal off air sources with solder, cork, and shellac, and to modify the choke disc with saw cuts and pliers. More "back-yard" engineering!

Over and above the design problems was the problem of nonconformity to design specifications. The first 1,660 Arrows and 268 Scouts left without the wheel hubs greased, and the same problem resurfaced in Scouts serial numbered 2000 through 2047! Some Arrows were shipped without removing the welding flux and acid from the gas and oil tanks, and this led to rust that could clog up oil passages. Failure to clean sealing surfaces during assembly resulted in leaking telescopic forks. Dealers had to partially disassemble the forks, clean them, and reinstall gaskets.

Mismatching of drive gears on some units resulted in very noisy valve gear train noise. The gears were made in two different styles, the difference being the pitch angle, a measurement of the geometrical relationship between engaging gears. Early Arrows had cam gears with a 20-degree pitch angle, and later Arrows had a 14-1/2-degree pitch angle. Some Scouts had 14-1/2-degree cam gears and others had a 20-degree pitch angle. Although

Changes on the 1951 Warrior were confined to the paint scheme.

117

the two types of gears had different part numbers and were shipped in separate boxes properly marked, the part numbers weren't marked on the gears. The later 14-1/2-degree gears were cadmium plated and the earlier 20-degree gears weren't, but the cadmium plating became less obvious after the gears had been in use. Lack of good factory records resulted in a salt and pepper application process. Most singles between serial numbers 1001 and 3485 had 20-degree teeth, but a few were supplied with 14-1/2-degree teeth. Nearly all twins had the 20-degree teeth gears, but a few had the other gears. Evidently, mismatching was occurring in the dealerships, because the factory had to issue instructions. Mechanics were told to place a 1/16-inch diameter drill between the teeth of a gear. If the gear could be rocked between the gear teeth, it was

a late 14-1/2-degree gear. If the drill fit tightly between the teeth, it was an early 20-degree gear.

Improper installation could also produce valvetrain noise. The valvetrain gears were supported by predrilled plain bearings. Sometimes the internal diameters of the bearings were distorted when the bearings were pressed into the cases. This was solved in late 1948 by precision boring the bearings after they had been pressed in.

The September 1948, *Business Week* published an optimistic article about Indian's postwar program. But also in September, at about the time that the solutions appeared at hand for the production and reliability problems of the Arrow and Scout, Rogers' projected lightweight revolution was given the death sentence by the British government's devaluation of the Pound

For 20 years, Max Bubeck campaigned this Indian vertical twin in California desert events. In 1955 he built this swinging-arm rear suspension. "That's when everybody started going by me. By then, everybody had swing arms." Bubeck rode this version to wins in the 1962 (500-mile) Greenhorn Enduro, the 1965 Gold Rush Enduro, and many other events.

Sterling from about $4 to about $3. This had the effect of lowering the price of the growing body of imported English motorcycle by about one-third. At the stroke of a pen, Indian's pricing went from competitive to uncompetitive. In November 1948, Indian released another 250 employees, leaving about 800 in the force. Employment was thus about half what had been projected as required to bring on board the new lineup of singles and vertical twins.

Laconia, June 1949 Vertical Twins Flunk Out

For the upcoming 1950 season, Indian was preparing 30.50-ci vertical twins that would debut under the model name "Warrior." Twenty-four preproduction Warriors were entered at the Laconia 100-mile national championship road race, and Indian placed its top riders on them. But only three of the 24 finished among the top 20 places! [*Motorcyclist* race results included only the first 20 finishers of the field of 49 riders.] The finishing riders listed were Bee Bee Smith (12th), Oscar Sherman (16th), and Bobby Baer (20th). Ed Kretz told me there were 12 "factory" riders, and that his bike and the other 11 all suffered magneto failure! These production magnetos were not the same as the successful prototype magnetos used in preproduction testing, according to Laconia veterans. The writer for *Motorcyclist* was that old Indian fan Ted Hodgdon who, looking at a field of 24 Indian vertical twin riders, actually had the nerve to mitigate the disaster by writing "Several 30.50 Indians were entered . . ." Several?

The Indian factory also tried to put a good face on the bad news. A writer under enough pressure will write almost anything, and staffer Dale Sayre rose to the considerable challenge and saved his job with this piece from the *Monday Morning Release*, Number 838 of July 4.

Twenty-three of the twenty-four Vertical Twin 30.50 mounted Indian competition riders unanimously declared and expressed their desire to return to Laconia again in 1950—Indian Vertical Twin 30.50 mounted. It became very apparent . . . that their maneuverability had it all over any other bike on the course . . . Unfortunately, lack of familiarity with the controls caused our Indian riders some concern. Quite a few of these men had never ridden a foot shift motorcycle until the week of the

race . . . At about the 10th lap Kretz came into his pit for a sparkplug change. Later he came in with a flat tire and still later with a broken chain . . . [Other riders] had pretty much the same luck . . . As the race progressed you could plainly see, and you could hear, too, that Indian riders were learning when to shift, and also how to come down through the gears . . .

Riders Ed Kretz, Lee Potter, and Oscar Sherman lent their names to the following statement in the press release:

Laconia was a test that all machines must endure before all of the bugs can be ironed out and it proved beyond a doubt that Indian has developed a machine that is destined to be the motorcycle of the world. Its handling, acceleration, and

Top racing stars in America's Class C (stock) game had to do much or even all of their own mechanical work. This is Bobby Hill getting his Sport Scout engine ready for the next race. Top riders were small but muscular. *Bobby Hill collection*

maneuverability were not excelled or even approached by any machine there. We feel that within two months there will be no motorcycle that will stay close to the Indian Warrior in competition or on the road.

One should probably cut the riders some slack, especially Kretz, who was also an Indian dealer and was facing the problem of how to sell Indian vertical twins to non-relatives. The "record-setting" Indian press release continued:

We must be realistic and recognize that this was the first appearance of the Vertical Twin 30.50 Indian Warriors in any race at all, not to mention in big time competition. Riders, dealers, and some factory people alike were astonished at the handling, top speed, and stamina of these 30.50 Warriors. There were no major mechanical failures at all; not an engine quit; frames and forks gave no trouble; clutches were as free and positive at the end of the race as they were at the start; and the engines were actually running even better.

"No major mechanical failures at all?" How is it that "engines were actually running even better," when 12 of them didn't have any sparks? If all that stuff—frames, forks, engines, clutches—was so great, how in the hell did Indian place only three riders in the top 20? Kretz confirmed the Warriors' good acceleration and their top speed in the mid-90s were all that was needed for the tight one-mile road course. So the absence of a representative number of places in the top 20 confirms sick motorcycles. Who, besides Kretz, either had his Warrior quit altogether, stop for repairs, or limp along off the pace? We may assume the top 12 factory-supported riders included some familiar names that were so conspicuously absent in the magazine article and the press release: Frenchy Castonguay, Woodsie Castonguay, Ted Edwards, Bobby Hill, Ed Kretz (we actually know he was there), and Johnny Spieglehoff. Five others were named in the press release: Billy Armstrong, Bill Tuman, Lee Potter, Muriel Pitcox, and Doc Savage. That, according to Kretz's story, leaves one other, and your guess is as good as mine.

Massive Production Doesn't Happen

Adding the stark fact of uncompetitive pricing to the production delays, cost over-runs, and quality control problems of the 1949 Torque models proved damning. Instead of manufacturing tens of thousands of the new Verticals, less

RUGGED, COMPACT and EXTREMELY MANEUVERABLE with small turning radius . . . accommodates machine gun or mortar for close-up infantry support; unexcelled r scouting and messenger work . . . commercially it affords speedier, more econom- deliveries especially in congested areas . . . farmers and sportsmen can go with quipment to places heretofore inaccessible except on horseback or on foot . . . the PATROL offers so much to so many for so little.

6 cu. ft. storage compartment beneath rear 2 man seat. stores meter collections, police equipment, ammunition. "wet" water tank sporting equipment. farm implements or goods for commercial delivery.

than 6,000 1949 models had left the new factory in East Springfield.

In April 1949, Ralph Rogers traveled to England and secured a $1.5 million loan from J. Brockhouse & Co., Ltd. To get the loan, Brockhouse was admitted to the Indian board of directors and chartered to set up and manage an independent distributing company called Indian Sales Corporation. Under the arrangement, the Indian Motocycle Company agreed to build new Indians and to sell them exclusively to Indian Sales, at specified prices. Indian Sales retained the exclusive Indian distribution rights so long as they ordered minimum specified quantities of new Indians. As the situation continued to sour, in November 1949, Indian Sales began distributing the following English motorcycles in the United States: AJS, Excelsior (no connection with the former American marque), Matchless (except in California), Norton, Royal Enfield, and Vincent.

Indian Tries to Make the Warrior Race-Ready

Sport Scout parts were no longer available in quantity, so the Indian engineering staff kept trying to develop a good racing motorcycle from the Warrior. Jack Armstrong relates:

I went to work for Indian in 1951. In '51 I started to ride the Indian Warrior. We tried to develop them for racing. I rode them on half-miles, miles, Langhorne, and Laconia. This was after that big (1949) fiasco they had with the Indian

Indian staffer Whitey Anderson posed for this sales literature shot. The vertical twin Patrol was offered in 1952 and 1953—after two-wheeled Scout descendants were out of production. This was Indian's last model with a right-side hand-shift. The Patrol featured a Borg-Warner clutch and transmission, plus a Crosley automobile differential.

121

Warriors. Walt Brown had some special cylinders cast up and some special heads cast up for the Warrior. Instead of them being diecast, they were sand cast. He had them cast up but he never had them machined because just at about that time they were thinking about dropping that program. It was a terrible program. So he gave me a set of the heads and a set of the cylinders, and I had them machined, and they were set up with twin carbs. The trouble with the stock diecast cylinders and cylinder heads was that they were too weak. Before we went to the special heads, we ran my motor on the dyno and it seemed to be moving around in the valve rocker area. We put a gauge on the heads and

Vintage competition is popular today. Californian Eric Vaughn has ridden this stroked 57-ci (about 930-cc) "stroker" Scout to over 131 miles per hour—over 133 miles per hour with a minimal front fairing. As of this writing, the engine is still fitted with a single carburetor, so it seems that even higher speeds may yet be achieved following additional development. Only Max Bubeck has ridden an unstreamlined Indian faster, turning over 135 miles per hour in 1948 on a "Chout" (Chief engine in a Series 101 Scout frame).

So we started to try to develop the Warrior as a competition bike, thinking that if we could, it may generate enough interest in it that it would help Indian. It just never worked out. It was a toy! It just wasn't an adequate motorcycle. I can remember sitting in the office, just before I ran Laconia, with Mr. Baker, one of the engineers. And I can remember telling him that regardless of what we did to this motorcycle from the bottom of the cylinders up, that from the bottom of the cylinders down, and the transmission, (it) just was not adequate for any type of prolonged racing. We had solved the magneto problem that they had with it. It used a Sport Scout magneto with an adapter on the end of it, and it worked out fine. It solved the ignition problem which was the primary problem when they first put out that whole batch and they went to Laconia and nobody finished. We had solved that problem. And it's probably just as well that they didn't, because if they had kept on running they would have run into the other problems. They would've run into the problem of the gearbox not being sturdy enough, brake problems. So, we worked with it for three years. If we pulled up the adequate horsepower, we couldn't get the staying power, and when we could get the staying power we couldn't get the horsepower. So it was just a bad deal all the way around.

1948-1954 The Wrecking Crew

The last Indian racing glory came to the throttle-twisting hands of three riders: Bobby Hill, Bill Tuman, and Ernie Beckman, the fabled Indian "Wrecking Crew." Together with their builders-tuners and helpers, Dick Gross (for Hill), Ernie "Smitty" Smith (for Tuman), and Art Hafer (for Beckman), they reaped a maximum of victories without significant support from the struggling Indian company. Help came instead from a handful of Indian dealers. Bobby Hill recalls:

Indian had about seven or eight dealers in the state of Ohio, and they picked out the most promising riders and set them up with bikes. But the dealers had to buy; it wasn't direct supply from the factory. And just because you had the bike, that didn't make it fast. They didn't give us travel money or anything like that from the factory. But when we would visit dealers, like we would go and visit Hap

determined that at 7,000 rpm to 7,200 rpm the rocker boxes were flexing up and down 40 to 50 thousandths of an inch. The sand-case heads were thicker in that area and stronger. They had made a frame for Woodsie (Castonguay) for running dirt track with the Indian Warrior, which he never did. They gave me that frame.

Jones on the [west] Coast, he would take care of you. He would put you up and service your car and get you gas, and you know, show you a good time while we were there.

Praise from a rival means a lot, and from a strong rival means even more. In that era, the unexcelled Harley-Davidson builder-tuner was Tom Sifton of San Jose, California. Sifton's motorcycles were always faster than all other Harleys, even those assembled in the Milwaukee racing department, and Sifton's riders Sam Arena, Larry Headrick, and Joe Leonard were of hall-of-fame caliber. Here's what Tom Sifton said about the Indian Wrecking Crew:

In 1951, they [the Wrecking Crew] were all out here again. At that time [Kenny] Eggars was riding my number-one [best] motorcycle, and he won easily. He beat the Indian crew and Dick Klamfoth [Norton]. The guys from down south [including Ed Kretz] were all riding Triumphs, and he beat them easily. Well, when we got back to Springfield, things had changed. The fact is, Hill beat us at Springfield.

You had three camps. You had Gross, and you had Tuman, and you had a fellow up around Detroit, Art Hafer. Those three guys put their heads together. Hafer understood valve springs and certain parts of valve action. Gross understood porting to some extent and was making cams. He was moving the valves farther, opening them farther than what any of them were. And Tuman's connection was through the oiling, the things that made a motorcycle last.

Well, they put their heads together and they came up with a motorcycle at Springfield and the following Sunday at the Milwaukee mile [one-mile track]. Hill had a little edge on us . . . and the stuff went fast.

Lightness of weight helped the Wrecking Crew, too. Sifton told me that every six or seven pounds removed was like adding one horsepower. Hap Jones received Bobby Hill's bike in a shipping crate. Jones said the loaded crate, including a spare tire and wheel, weighed less than a stock KR Harley-Davidson on the starting line!

Bobby Hill remembered his Indians as motorcycles that seemed to always have more revolutions in reserve:

One thing we had with the Indians, it seemed like at the end of the straightaway, when most motors would peak, we never seemed to peak. We could always get that extra surge. There was never this lull in an engine, where cams come

in and out, and this and that. We never had that with the Indians.

A staple of Hill's racer was the fitting of ball bearings to the crankshaft. Hill's racer for one-mile track races also had a special valve drive, and Harley-Davidson connecting rods were used! These bikes were "cheaters," since under A.M.A. rules these would not have been permitted. But "everybody" cheated to some extent, or felt their rivals were. Hill recalls:

Dick set up ball bearings. Everything had ball bearings. We had four-cam [i.e., four separate cam lobes instead of two lobes timing both inlet and exhaust for each cylinder]. Everybody knew we had that. There was nothing too great about that. It was just [about] knowing where you wanted your valves to open. We always used Harley rods. But as far as having our bore and stroke and everything, we were legal. We ran a "legal" bike; we just tried to make them run a little better.

"Obsolete" Victories

The Wrecking Crew won many races on what I like to call the "twilight" Scouts, since they were raced after the "sunset" of Scout production. Bear in mind that in the era there were only about 10 national championship races per year, less than half the total in recent years. The three riders won numerous regional races, races that in today's environment would be called national championships. Also, when they were not in their Wrecking Crew mode, Hill and Tuman won some road races during this period on Nortons. Here's a summary of Indian Wrecking Crew national championships.

1950: Tuman, Des Moines, Iowa, 1/2-mile track, 5-mile national championship. Tuman, Reading, Pennsylvania, 1/2-mile track, 8 miles.

1951: Hill, Springfield, Illinois, 1-mile track, 25-miles, winner got the No. 1 one plate, record time. Hill, Milwaukee, Wisconsin, 1-mile track, 15 miles, record time.

1952: Beckman, Columbus, Ohio, 1/2-mile track, 10 miles. Beckman, Williams Grove, Pennsylvania, 1/2-mile track, 8 miles. Hill, Richmond, Virginia, 1/2-mile track, 10 miles. Hill, Syracuse, New York, 1-mile track, 10 miles. Hill, Springfield, Illinois, 1-mile track, 25 miles (kept No. 1 plate). Hill, Indianapolis, Indiana, 1-mile track, 5 miles. Tuman, Bay Meadows, California, 1-mile track, 20 miles, track record.

1953: Tuman, Springfield, Illinois, 1-mile track, 25 miles, won No. 1 plate. Beckman,

Williams Grove, Pennsylvania, 1/2-mile track, 8 miles, last racing national championship for Indian. Tuman, mythical No. 1 rider per *Cycle* magazine proposed seasonal points; similar system adopted by the A.M.A. the following season.

Not included in the previous summary was Bill Tuman's non-national win on the Saint Paul, Minnesota, 1/2-mile track, in which he set an 8-mile record. During 1954 and 1955, Beckman, Hill, and Tuman placed second and third in several national championships before abandoning the iron redskins. Hill and Tuman carried the prestigious No. 1 plate on their Indians (and Nortons) in 1952, 1953, and 1954, each being the year following their victories at the Springfield, Illinois, 25-mile national championship. Ironically, race fans watched Tuman circle the tracks on his No. 1 Indian during 1954, the year following the cessation of Indian production.

1950–952 Closure

As noted earlier, Ralph Rogers didn't completely control the Indian Motocycle Company, but was instead backed by a financial group to which Rogers was heavily indebted. The group included the Atlas Corp., the Chemical Bank, the Marine Midland Banks, and a latecomer, the English John Brockhouse group, which Rogers had recruited in a desperate bid to keep Indian afloat. In January 1950, as a result of the Torque models fiasco, Rogers was ousted as company president and replaced by John Brockhouse.

Leftover 1949 Arrows and Scouts were cosmetically altered and offered up as 1950 models. The company stoutly claimed both these models would continue in production, but these were the last of the 13-ci single-cylinder Arrows and 26-ci twin-cylinder Scouts. In terms of new Indian motorcycles, the proud "Scout" name thus came to an end.

In late 1950, an off-road vertical twin was introduced as the Warrior TT. Numerous details adapted the Warrior TT ideally to American TT racing and off-road enduro events. One of the more appealing aspects was that the bike came stripped for action. Competition riders didn't have to waste money and time buying and then removing unnecessary lights and generator, and replacing unsuitable fenders. The basic off-road goodies were also there, including a rugged skid plate to protect the engine and transmission, plus various features that improved water resistance.

The road-going Warrior model was offered in the 1950 and 1951 seasons, with minor cosmetic differences. Patient and determined factory staffer Walt Brown still had hopes of developing the Warrior into a competitive racer, and had done preliminary planning for a more robust lower end and transmission to match up with the sand-cast experimental cylinders and cylinder heads. Several prototype 1952 road model Warriors were assembled in two major variants, one with a typically compact frame and the other with a larger frame that elevated the fuel tank several inches higher above the cylinder heads. The latter was in response to criticisms by riders and particularly by police departments that the earlier Warrior models were too small for comfort. Indian advertised the 1952 Warrior road model in the April issue of *Cycle*, which was distributed in March, and for which advertising was laid out in February. Somewhere in that time frame, Indian decided to cancel plans for the 1952 road model Warrior, which likewise killed any chances of special racing Warriors incorporating Walt Brown's ideas.

The Warrior TT continued to be assembled and distributed during the year. In total, only about 6,000 vertical-twin or Torque models were built. For 1953 no two-wheeled Warriors were built, but the company offered up a three-wheeled version for police and delivery duty, building perhaps a couple dozen. Along with the 1953 80-ci Chiefs, these were the last of the continuous line of American-built Indians, bringing to an end a once-proud tradition dating back to 1901. Staffers who looked back on the great days of new Sport Scouts coming off the line and battling on even terms with rival race teams maintained a glimmer of hope. Among the prototype models in the factory at the end of production was a motorcycle consisting of a Sport Scout V-twin engine in a modified Warrior frame.

The Magic and Illusion of the Scout

The original 1920 Scout was very successful, but part of that success came at the expense of other Indian models, particularly the big-twin Chief. The first Scout, and the companion Chief, did not deliver a serious blow to Harley-Davidson in terms of overall sales, yet there was no question that the Scouts of the early 1920s were head and shoulders above the rival Harley-Davidson Sport, which was thus terminated. The 1927 "Scout 45" brought unexpected new power and speed, helping in the rivalry with Harley, but regrettably also challenging the sales of the Indian Chief. The Scout 45 met a worthy rival in the comparable Super-X 45, but the Excelsior product was doomed by the weakness of the manufacturer. The Super-X 45 was built in too small numbers to be visible in the everyday world.

Bobby Hill in action. Hill, Bill Tuman, and Ernie Beckman formed the Indian "Wrecking Crew" in the early 1950s, sharing among them several national championship titles. Hill rode with the No. 1 plate in 1952 and 1953, following his wins of the 1951 and 1952 Springfield, Illinois, 25-mile titles (one-mile track). Tuman won Springfield in 1953 and rode as No. 1 in 1954—when Indians were no longer in production. *Bobby Hill collection*

Along came the Series 101 Scout in 1928, a model with something for everybody. The 101 might have restored Indian to production parity with Harley-Davidson, but the 101 came along at a time when financiers were more interested in manipulating the value of Indian stock than in building Indian motorcycles. Old-timers recalled that Series 101 Scout production never caught up with demand during its production seasons of 1928 through 1931. Among those who rode and sold Indians during the era, the Series 101 Scout is the most fondly remembered of all models. Then came two years, 1932 and 1933, of middleweight "wandering," when Indian's low-end models were outgrowths of a discarded 1920s single-cylinder model.

With the Sport Scouts of 1934 through 1939, Indian reached supremacy in American motorcycle racing. Sport Scouts never sold like the original Scouts and Series 101 Scouts, but their role as a successful standard bearer cast a halo glow over the other Indians and served the company well. When World War II brought its motorcycle needs in late 1941, the Sport Scout and the smaller Thirty-fifty were transformed into suitable military models that were used through 1945. The melancholy postwar history included the cancellation of the anticipated new Sport Scout. The choice of the "Scout" name for the 1949 vertical twin perhaps signified the huge hope that was part

of Roger's equation, a hope born of the illustrious history behind the name. But this was a hope that was not to be fulfilled, largely due to international finances beyond Indian's control. Brightening the last years were the exploits of the Indian Wrecking Crew, which saw Indian as "No. 1" for the seasons of 1951, 1952, and 1953, and carrying that honor forward through 1954.

Had Indian been too successful with the first Scouts? Had Indian been mystified by the "holy grail" of motorcycle factories, the hope that an "everyman" model could skyrocket sales by reaching into the vast sideline and converting secret admirers into motorcyclists? No, not guilty. The Scouts, the Series 101 Scouts, the little twins of various names, the Motoplane, the Sport Scouts, and, in a way even the vertical twins had been built because they *had* to be built. It was part of the "game" of being a motorcycle company, to seek converts, to race, to set records, to march off to war, to race again, and, finally, to take the big gamble, a gamble that might have seen Indian again becoming America's largest motorcycle company. It is not for timid people to race motorcycles, or even to ride them on the streets and highways, so why should timid people run motorcycle companies? We wish things had turned out differently. But we're in love with the struggle. That's partly why we love our old Indian motorcycles so much. "You can't wear out an Indian Scout!—Indian Wins Again!"

Index

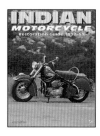
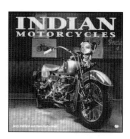
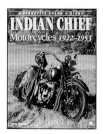
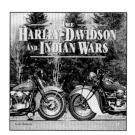
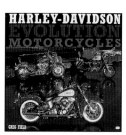
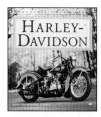

ORDERS, DECORATIONS AND BADGES OF THE SOCIALIST REPUBLIC OF VIETNAM
and the National Front for the Liberation of South Vietnam

Edward J. Emering

Schiffer Military History
Atglen, PA

Dedication:
To my friend and wife, Cali

Acknowledgements:
To Gerry Schooler, Ned Broderick, John Sylvester, Jr., Peter Aitken, CDR Frank Brown, USN. And to the artists . . . from the National Vietnam Veterans Art Museum, Phillip Pelipada and Chuck Zimmaro.

Book Design by Ian Robertson.

Printed in China.
ISBN: 0-7643-0143-8

We are interested in hearing from authors with book ideas on related topics.

Published by Schiffer Publishing Ltd.
77 Lower Valley Road
Atglen, PA 19310
Phone: (610) 593-1777
FAX: (610) 593-2002
E-mail: Schifferbk@aol.com
Please write for a free catalog.
This book may be purchased from the publisher.
Please include $2.95 postage.
Try your bookstore first.

PREFACE

The field of Vietnamese communist decorations has long been a source of puzzlemment to Western scholars, historians and collectors. A standard reference work simply did not exist, and much of what was published – while well-intentioned – only served to exacerbate the problem through faulty identifications, erroneous translations, and the like.

Happily, this situation has now been rectified by Edward J. Emering, a Chicago-based decorated veteran and scholar whose 25 years of research into the subject resulted in the publication of this book, which is destined to become the "Bible" on Vietnamese communist awards.

Authoritative in scope, and lavishly illustrated, the book covers the establishment and evolution of Viet Minh, Viet Cong and North Vietnamese awards, as well as those retained and utilized by the present-day Socialist Republic of Vietnam. Of particular interest, are many of the obsolete awards and badges, official as well as unofficial, which appear here for the first time and are covered in depth.

Ed Emering is to be commended for his pioneering efforts in this field. He has succeeded in creating a book that fills a long-recognized void and will appeal to scholar and layman alike.

CDR. F.C. Brown, USN
Hamilton Twp., New Jersey
April 1996

INTRODUCTION

This work was encouraged in large part by receipt and translation of a document titled: *Orders and Decorations*, issued by the Socialist Republic of Vietnam (SRV) Institute of Orders in Hanoi. It catalogs the official 18 Orders and 14 Decorations issued by both the SRV as well as the National Front for the Liberation of South Vietnam (MTDGPMNVN or NLF as used herein), which had previously been postured as an independent political movement. Although issued by the NLF, these awards are worn by SRV military personnel, who staffed most of the NLF units following the 1968 Tet Offensive.

While these 32 medals represent the current official version of the SRV's award system, they by no means should be interpreted as comprising all awards bestowed by either the SRV or the NLF. I have been an avid collector of the awards issued by the SRV and its predecessors for years. I have literally hundreds of diverse SRV and NLF awards and badges in my collection. These pieces date from the mid-1940s through the current post-war period. Many are documented in the subsequent sections of this book.

During this 50 year period, the SRV award system has undergone numerous changes in both scope and design. In particular, the Orders reflect these changes most dramatically. In most cases, such as the Liberation Army Order, both the Order and the corresponding Decoration are quite similar. In other examples however, such as with the Liberation Order and Decoration, the new version of the Order looks nothing like the Decoration, which has remained unchanged from its original design. Another striking example of design change took place in the Resistance Order, which was originally struck in the form of a cross. No information is available on the appearance of the corresponding, original Resistance Decoration, if any ever existed. The current Resistance Decoration parallels the redesigned Order. Finally, a previously high ranking, not to mention striking Decoration, the Brass Fortress of the Fatherland

(THANH DONG TO-QUOC), does not appear among the "official" awards of the SRV, as reflected in the aforementioned publication.

Where it is noted that an Order is awarded in classes, the Soviet style pentagonal suspension ribbon is usually marked by the presence of small gold stars: three for first class, two for second, and one for third. In other cases, the ribbon reflects a variation in the number of contrasting stripes. Examples of this ribbon variation include: the Liberation Army Order, the Soldier of Liberation Order, the Order of the Soldier of Glory and the Victory Order. Only three of the official Decorations (Victory, Liberation and Resistance) are awarded in classes. In these instances, two small gold stars on the hero style suspension ribbon indicate first class; one indicates second class.

Orders are worn arranged on the left breast. The Gold Star Order and the three "Hero" Decorations (Labor, People's Armed Forces and Liberation Army) are worn centered above all other Orders on the left breast. The obsolete Brass Fortress of the Fatherland was also worn in this position, but has also been observed being worn on the right breast in more recent years. All other Decorations, along with political medals and campaign badges, are worn on the right breast, even the two domestic Decorations (the Banner of Resolution for Victory and Security of the Fatherland) which resemble Orders. NLF members wore their political badges on the left breast, along with any Orders which they had earned. Decorations were worn on the right breast. A third award, the Friendship Decoration, which also resembles an Order, is only awarded to foreign recipients.

Although the hierarchy of most of the SRV's Orders and Decorations remain a mystery, a high ranking Peoples Army of Vietnam (PAVN) colonel confirmed during a May 1965 interrogation by his ARVN captors that the following precedence existed: 1.) Gold Star;

2.) Ho Chi Minh Order; 3.) Independence Order; and 4.) Labor Order. These were considered "special" awards and as such ranked above "service" awards.

Orders and Decorations are rarely seen group mounted as they would be in other countries, the former Soviet Union included. Some senior PAVN officers have been observed with their awards neatly mounted, but in most cases they are pinned haphazardly to the uniform blouse.

It should also be noted that one Order and one Decoration bear the title, "Labor." In many cases, even though available to civilian workers, these have been bestowed on military personnel, since the PAVN is fully integrated into SRV society. This extends to the PAVN's involvement in both staffing and managing industrial and agricultural enterprises. These labor awards have also been liberally bestowed on foreign recipients.

My interest in this subject matter dates back to personal experiences in the late 1960s, and was heightened by my return to Vietnam in 1993. I have always been motivated by the "thrill of the hunt." Seeking out the diverse and obscure awards of a generally insular society has proven to be quite a challenge. Couple this with a feeling that it may be considered patriotic to the Vietnamese vendor to fool the Western buyer and the cards are stacked against the uninitiated collector.

The diplomatic recognition of the SRV in 1995 by the United States will open the barriers of this previously closed nation to Western visitors. As a result, it can be anticipated that the once scarce supply of SRV medals will continue to become more abundant, a trend which began several years ago when U.S. veterans began returning there. As it does, one might also expect the flow of imitations and cannibalized material (the use of disparate suspensions and planchets, i.e., the main part of the medal) to increase. This is particularly true of material emanating from the Saigon markets.

This work is being published to aid both the serious collector as well as the curious visitor to identify and verify the authenticity and accuracy of the SRV medals. Even if prices for these medals should decrease, a mistake could still be costly. Exceptions to this trend would be the Gold Star Order, the Ho Chi Minh Order, the Independence Order, and some of the older, official medals, which are no longer being struck. My expereince has been that prices for these senior awards have been escalating rapidly.

Chapter 1

Official Orders & Decorations

1. Gold Star Order

This simple medal, established on June 6, 1947, is the highest honor conferred by the SRV on both individuals and units. It is equivalent to the Hero of the Soviet Union medal, although it in no way matches the quality or workmanship of its Soviet counterpart. During his 1965 interrogation, a PAVN colonel confirmed that this Order had only been conferred once. It had also been awarded to Ho Chi Minh, who had refused it until final victory was achieved. As of 1974, only two of these Orders had been awarded. One to Ho Chi Minh and the second to Vice President Ton Duc Thang, who received his Gold Star Order from Ho Chi Minh in August, 1958. Ton Duc Thang eventually succeeded Ho on his death. Although a total of 16 Gold Stars have been awarded to date, the only positively known recipients include: Ho Chi Minh, Ton Duc Thang, Leonid Brezhnev and Aleksei Kosygin, who both received their awards in June, 1980; and the famous SRV military leader, Senior General Vo Nguyen Giap, who has often been photographed in uniform, wearing only the Gold Star Order.

It is also widely believed (but unconfirmed) that the Gold Star Order was also presented to PAVN General Tran Ba Thanh, who served as a ARVN officer on the South Vietnamese Prime Minister's staff during the war and provided invaluable intelligence to Hanoi. It is believed that he alone was responsible for the failed Son Tay prison raid, which attempted to rescue captive U.S. military personnel.

The planchet itself is a raised, five-pointed, solid gold star, measuring approximately 1 1/2" from point to point. The back is decorated with a raised wreath of two laurel branches. The medal is neither numbered nor named as might be typical in other countries of the world for such a high honor. The pin device is a simple bent wire.

The Order is worn on the left breast, centered above all other Orders. There is no corresponding service ribbon. Counterfeits have been observed, but the laurel leaves on the reverse were not present.

Brass Fortress Order.

The Gold Star Order Reverse.

2. Independence Order

Established on June 6, 1947, this medal was awarded in three classes to units and individuals for special service to the State. It is one of the most decorative and elaborate awards of the SRV. The brightly designed enamel center with white, red, blue and yellow is inscribed, DOC-LAP (Independence). It is among the more difficult awards to obtain.

The Independence Order.

Ho Chi Minh Order.

3. Ho Chi Minh Order

This award was established on June 6, 1947 and was revised to its current style on August 28, 1981. Since its revision, it is only issued in one class to both individuals and units. As pointed out by John Sylvester Jr. in his monograph, this medal would appear to be equivalent to the Soviet Order of Lenin, which was awarded in tandem with the Hero of the Soviet Union medal. There is currently no verification of this fact relative to the SRV system of awards, although the criteria for awarding the Gold Star Order and the Ho Chi Minh Order seem to be remarkably similar. The major exception is that the criteria for this award makes specific reference to the "revolutionary cause" of the people. Statistics indicate that while this Order is indeed rare, it has been awarded far more frequently than the Gold Star.

The well decorated PAVN Major General Vo Bam, who had rear echelon responsibility for the Ho Chi Minh Trail, pictured on his eightieth birthday. Note the Ho Chi Minh Order worn on the left center and the Victory Order 1st Class with green edge stripes also on the left. Courtesy of Gerry Schooler.

4. Fatherland Order

This award was established on September 23, 1963 and awarded by the NLF to units giving special service in the effort to liberate the south. It was awarded in one class. It is a ten- pointed gold star, which features a smaller five-pointed star surrounded by a shock of grain and a toothed gear with the inscription, TO-QUOC (Fatherland).

Fatherland Order.

Victory Order.

5. Brass Fortress Order

Established on September 23, 1963, this award of the NLF was bestowed in three classes on individuals and units for superior service in liberating the south. The five-pointed gold star with a smaller central star is inscribed, THANH-DONG (Brass Fortress).

On September 2, 1977, the Council of Ministers authorized the granting of this Order to units and individuals, who played key roles in the Spring, 1975 General Offensive and had not yet received an award for such service.

6. Military Exploit Order

Awarded in three classes to both units and individuals for outstanding performance in combat, this Order was established on May 15, 1947. It is one of the SRV's original awards. There are numerous photographs of PAVN unit flags adorned with this medal. The collector should note that many examples of this Order are missing the small gold wreath which links the planchet to the suspension ribbon. This is clearly an essential piece of the award. The red enamel center features a smaller five-pointed star, which is surrounded by the inscription, HUAN CHUONG QUAN CONG (Order of Military Achievement).

On March 6, 1979, President Ton Duc Thang awarded this Order to 48 units and seven individuals for their roles in the border conflict with China. It is interesting to note that the first and second class awards of this Order are reserved for smaller units. Battalion size and larger units are only eligible for third class awards.

Military Exploit Order.

Liberation Exploit Order.

7. Liberation Exploit Order

The NLF equivalent of the Military Exploit Order, it was established on September 23, 1963. It was also awarded in three classes on the same basis as the Military Exploit Order for combat action in the south. Again, note the presence of the essential small gold linking wreath. The inscription on this Order reads, QUAN CONG GIAI PHONG (Military Achievement Liberation). Recipients were also accorded the appellation Hero of the Liberation Front.

Bi Nang Thak of the Raglay Trible, Comissar of the Bak-Ai District and Hero of the National Liberation Front, wearing the Liberation Exploit Order. Courtesy of F.C. Brown.

8. Labor Order
Established on May 1, 1950, this medal is awarded in three classes to individuals and groups for outstanding intellectual or labor intensive accomplishments. Remember, the PAVN's role in the labor force elevates this to a quasi-military award. Early strikes of this award bear a serial number on the otherwise plain reverse. Its design is also highly decorative, featuring a gold star on a red enamel center surrounded by gold. The red enamel banner at the bottom reads, VIET NAM.

It has been awarded to various teams of Chinese experts, who assisted with the building of a label printing house in Vin Phu Province; the expansion of a fertilizer plant in Ha Bac Province; and the building of a medical appliance factory in Bac Thai. It was also presented to the Cuban members of the Ho Chi Minh International Builders Brigade.

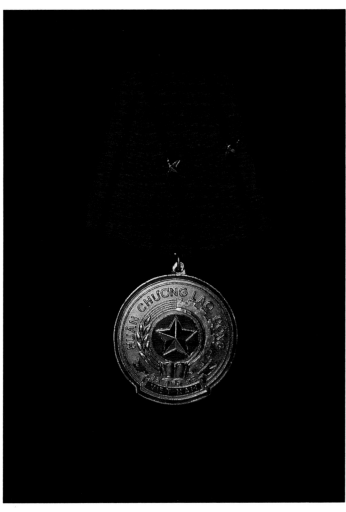

Labor Order.

Liberation Army Order.

9. Liberation Army Order
Established on February 2, 1958, this medal was awarded in three classes to individuals serving in the armed forces prior to the August 1945 Revolution. During this period, the Viet Minh, under Ho Chi Minh's leadership, attempted to fill the political void created by the defeat of the Japanese occupation forces at the end of World War II. Recipients were also required to have continued their army service until February 2, 1958, or, for at least five years. They must not have committed any serious errors during their service.

10. Victory Order

Established on February 2, 1958, this medal was awarded in three classes to soldiers serving in the PAVN between 1946 and 1954. It commemorates the army's victory in La Guerre d'Indochine, which culminated with defeat of the French Occupation Forces at the battle of Dien Bien Phu in May, 1954. Award of this Order was based on both length of army service, as well as good conduct during such period. Versions of this medal with both a gilt center as well as the official red enamel center are known to exist. The various classes

of this Order are denoted by the number of stripes on the pentagonal suspension ribbon and not by the presence of small gold stars. The first class award was reserved for personnel at the regimental or division level. The second class award was for personnel at the company, platoon or squad level. Third class awards were for non-commissioned officers and enlisted men. It is inscribed, CHIEN THANG (Victory). All classes have a thin green stripe along each side of the ribbon.

Soldier of Liberation Order.

Resolution for Victory Order.

11. Resolution for Victory Order

This was another of the NLF awards for units and individuals who were separated from their families while involved in the liberation of the south. It was established on August 9, 1965 and awarded in three classes. The first class version of the Order was awarded to

PAVN Colonel General Tran Van Tra, commander of NLF forces in Saigon during the entire war against the Americans. It was also widely awarded to personnel who participated in the Spring, 1975, General Offensive.

12. Combatant Order

Also referred to as the Meritorious Military Service Order, this medal is awarded to military personnel and units in three classes. It was established May 15, 1947 and is one of the SRV's original awards. It is given for exploits against an enemy in combat situations. It is another of those medals, frequently observed adorning unit flags. The original version was inscribed, VIETNAM DAN-CHU CONG-HOA (Vietnam Democratic Republic). This progressed to HUAN CHUONG CHIEN SI (Combatants Order) and eventually to its current version, HUAN CHUONG CHIEN CONG (Feat of Arms Order). This Order is only awarded to officers, "heroes," high ranking PAVN personnel, members of Sapper (special forces) units and battalion size and larger units.

Combatant Order.

Liberation War Exploit Order.

13. Liberation War Exploit Order

Awarded by the NLF to units and individuals for outstanding participation in armed combat in the south, this Order was established on September 23, 1963. The five-pointed, hollow silver star features the NLF flag on a central gold disc. It was awarded in three classes. Its inscription reads, CHIEN-CONG GIAI-PHONG (Armed Achievements Liberation).

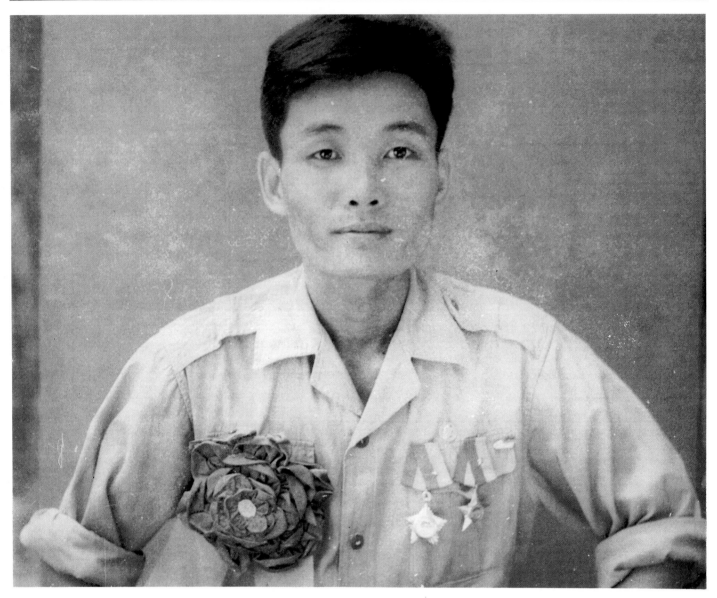

NLF Officer wearing the Liberation Exploit Order 3rd Class (left) and the Liberation War Exploit Order 3rd Class (right). Courtesy of F.C. Brown.

14. Resistance Order

Established on August 20, 1948, this Order was awarded in three classes to PAVN units and individuals for meritorious military service or service in support of the resistance against the French, between 1946 and 1954, and against the South Vietnamese and eventually, their American allies between 1954 and 1975. The obsolete version of this Order was observed being worn by a mother, who lost one son in the conflict against the French, and a second son in the conflict against the Americans. She was also wearing the current version of this Order. It is speculated that the design change occurred sometime after the war against the French ended in 1954 and that the new design has been awarded since the start of the Second Indochina War.

Resistance Order.

Liberation Order.

15. Liberation Order

Another NLF award, this Order was established on August 9, 1965, for units and individuals serving the cause of resistance and liberation in the south either in combat, production or some official capacity. Like the Order of Resolution for Victory, it was also awarded to families separated by the resistance and liberation efforts in the south. It was awarded in three classes and is also a modernized version of the obsolete form of the Order. The five- pointed gold star features the inscription, GIAI PHONG (Liberation).

This award was also authorized for presentation to units and individuals, who distinguished themselves during the Spring, 1975 General Offensive. It was also presented to families, whose relatives joined the "revolutionary ranks," during the Offensive.

16. *Order of the Soldier of Glory*

Established on September 16, 1961, this Order is given to PAVN personnel for long periods of meritorious service after July 20, 1954. Awarded in three classes, the over-sized, hollow, silver star (2") bears the official flag of the SRV on a central gold disc. The flag is inscribed, QUYET THANG (Resolved to Win). The medal also bears the inscription, CHIEN SI VE-VANG (Soldier of Glory), on a red ribbon at the bottom of the central disc. Requirements for the first class award are nine years of meritorious service. The second and third class awards require seven and five years of discipline-free service, respectively.

Order of the Soldier of Glory.

The Gold Star Order Obverse.

17. *Soldier of Liberation Order*

Awarded by the NLF to individuals who participated in the liberation of the south, this Order was established on July 6, 1966. There is only one class of this Order. The red ribbon features three light blue stripes in the center. The inscription below the NLF flag reads, CHIEN SI GIAI PHONG (Soldier of Liberation).

18. Friendship Order

Established on January 28, 1977, this Order is bestowed upon foreigners who have aided the SRV in its resistance and rebuilding efforts. It is awarded in one class only. An example of this Order was acquired at a Moscow flea market in 1994 and is most likely of Czechoslovakian origin, where these medals were manufactured during the 1960s.

On May 10, 1977, the Friendship Order was presented to Gianni Giadresco, head of the Italy-Vietnam Committee, for organizing Italian support for Vietnam. In a number of other instances, it has been awarded to foreign recipients in conjunction with the award of the Labor Order.

Army Museum Tower, Hanoi, circa 1882. It once served as a French Fortress. By Charles P. Zimmaro.

Friendship Order.

Youth conference in Hanoi, circa 1973 with PAVN student and two highly decorated National Liberation Front soldiers. Courtesy of F.C. Brown.

19. Fatherland Commemorative Decoration

Established on January 26, 1946, this medal was awarded in one class to PAVN units and individuals who served in the Revolution of 1945. The round disc with a bust of Ho Chi Minh is suspended hero-style from a red ribbon surrounded by a gold frame. Although the Decoration bears a resemblance to the Ho Chi Minh Order, its restrictive purpose is quite distinct from that of the more senior Ho Chi Minh Order.

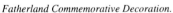

Fatherland Commemorative Decoration.

Labor Hero Decoration.

20. Labor Hero Decoration

Established on May 3, 1952 and revised on January 27, 1970, this medal recognizes groups and individuals who have been awarded the honorary title, "Hero of Labor." It is awarded in one class to military as well as civilian recipients and is worn on the left breast above all other Orders, except the Gold Star Order. Its rank is equivalent to the People's Armed Forces Hero and the Liberation Armed Forces Hero Decorations. In November 1964, it was awarded to Soviet cosmonauts at a ceremony in Moscow, marking the 47th anniversary of the Russian Revolution.

21. People's Armed Forces Hero

Established on May 2, 1952 and revised on January 27, 1970, this award for heroism ranks just below the Gold Star Order and is bestowed upon PAVN members with the honorary title of "Hero of the People's Armed Forces." The Decoration has been illustrated with a small gold star on the red suspension ribbon bar, but it has never been otherwise observed with the small gold star. It is awarded in one class only and is worn on the left breast above all Orders, except the Gold Star Order. Photographs indicate that this award may be worn by mothers and/or wives of posthumous recipients.

On October 17, 1976, the SRV National Assembly conferred this Decoration on 97 units and 20 individuals for outstanding exploits in the Second Indochina War. It would seem reasonable to infer that these units and individuals had previously earned the Military Exploit Order.

People's Armed Forces Hero Decoration.

Liberation Armed Forces Hero Decoration.

22. Liberation Armed Forces Hero

This is the NLF equivalent of the Hero of the People's Armed Forces Decoration. It was established on September 3, 1963. It is extremely rare. It was awarded prior to 1976 in one class only and worn above all other NLF awards. Again, its reasonable to infer that recipients had previously earned the Liberation Exploit Order.

23. Liberation Army Decoration

This PAVN Decoration tracks the Order of the same name, in both purpose and appearance. It is awarded in one class, suspended from a red ribbon bar with a single central yellow stripe.

Liberation Army Decoration.

Resistance Decoration.

24. Resistance Decoration

This PAVN Decoration tracks the Order of the same name. It is awarded in two classes, which are denoted by small gold stars on the red suspension ribbon with two yellow stripes at either end. Two stars denote first class; one star second class.

25. Soldier of Glory Decoration

This PAVN Decoration tracks the Order of the same name. The star device is considerably smaller than that of the Order. It is awarded in one class, suspended from a red ribbon bar with a central yellow stripe. Presentation of this Decoration requires three to five years of discipline-free service in the PAVN.

Soldier of Glory Decoration.

26. Victory Decoration

This Decoration tracks the Order of the same name. It is awarded in two classes and exists with both the official red enamel as well as a gilt center. It is suspended from a red ribbon bar with one central yellow stripe. The planchet is considerably smaller than that of the corresponding Order. It was given to those personnel who did not meet the minimum five year service requirement for award of the Order, but who had served for at least three years.

Victory Decoration (official version).

Victory Decoration (gilt version).

27. Liberation Decoration

This NLF Decoration tracks the Order of the same name. Interestingly enough, this Decoration closely resembles the obsolete version of the Order. The Decoration bears the NLF flag along with the inscription, GIAI PHONG (Liberation). The suspension ribbon bar is light blue at each of the edges and red in the center. The decoration is awarded in two classes as noted by the presence of one or two small gold stars on the suspension bar.

Liberation Decoration.

Resolution for Victory Decoration.

28. Resolution for Victory Decoration

This NLF Decoration, established on August 9, 1965, was awarded in only one class to individuals separated from their families while participating in the resistance and liberation of the south. Although noticeably dissimiliar in appearance, it would seem directly linked to the Order of the same name. It was widely awarded to personnel participating in the Spring, 1975, General Offensive. It has been observed in bronze and flat silver finishes in addition to the official gilt finish.

This particular Decoration also seems related to at least three additional known NLF Decorations, none of which are listed as official by the Institute of Orders. For this reason, it is believed that several examples of this particular Decoration exist with mismatched suspension ribbon bars from the other three similar awards as a result of "slap dash" efforts by the sellers to assemble diverse pieces. Because several of the like Decorations may have been awarded in multiple classes, some confusion also exists regarding the award of this particular Decoration. I feel relatively certain that this Decoration is issued in one class only with a single star on the ribbon bar. In private correspondence, John Sylvester raises the issue that this Decoration has, to date, not been observed being worn in any photographs of PAVN or NLF personnel. I concur with this observation. This Decoration and the three like awards may never have been actually issued, since their display has never been observed.

29. Soldier of Liberation Decoration

This NLF Decoration tracks the Order of the same name. It was awarded in one class. Although like the preceding Decoration, examples have been seen with the half red, half blue ribbon bar bearing one or two small stars. This has led to the speculation that this Decoration was also awarded in multiple classes. Again, this is likely just another example of "slap dash" on the part of the sellers.

Soldier of Liberation Decoration.

Banner of Resolution for Victory Decoration.

30. Banner of Resolution for Victory Decoration

Established on October 27, 1984, this Decoration serves to recognize longevity and is bestowed upon personnel who have served the PAVN for 25 years or more. It is awarded in only one class and is worn on the right breast even though it more closely resembles an Order.

PAVN Sr. Colonel Le Trong Tam, who worked closely with MGen. Vo on the Ho Chi Minh Trail. Note the position of the Banner of Resolution for Victory Decoration, awarded for longevity, on the right, even though it resembles an Order. Courtesy of Gerry Schooler.

31. Security of the Fatherland Decoration

Another longevity award, this Decoration, established on August 13, 1985, was given to government officials, PAVN members and security service personnel with more than 25 years of service. It is awarded in only one class and is also worn on the right breast, like the preceding Decoration. The large gold star bears the SRV flag and an inscription that reads, VI AN NINH TO-QUOC (For Security of the Fatherland).

Security of the Fatherland Decoration.

Friendship Decoration.

32. Friendship Decoration

Awarded to foreigners, who have aided the Vietnamese in defending and building their country, this Decoration was established on June 20, 1960. It is awarded in one class and is the only other official SRV award, in addition to the Labor Order, which has been observed with a serial number on the reverse. The round disc is of very solid construction. About 20,000 of these Decorations were awarded during the Second Indochina War. The example of this Decoration in the author's collections appears to be of Eastern European origin based on its quality of manufacture and mounting on a rigid Soviet style frame.

The SRV Pyramid of Honor

Based on my analysis of the SRV's official awards and the interrogations of several captured PAVN soldiers, I have developed the following pyramid of honor:

Senior Awards
Gold Star Order
Ho Chi Minh Order
Independence Order

PAVN Awards for PAVN Service
People's Armed Forces Hero
Military Exploit Order
Resistance Order & Decoration
Combatant Order
Soldier of Glory Order & Decoration
Victory Order & Decoration
Liberation Army Order & Decoration
Fatherland Commemorative Decoration

PAVN Awards for NLF Service
Liberation Armed Forces Hero

Liberation Exploit Order
Liberation War Exploit Order
Brass Fortress Order
Fatherland Order
Liberation Order & Decoration
Resolution for Victory Order & Decoration
Soldier of Liberation Order & Decoration

Longevity Awards
Banner of Resolution for Victory
Security of the Fatherland

Labor Awards
Labor Order
Labor Hero

Foreign Awards
Friendship Order & Decoration

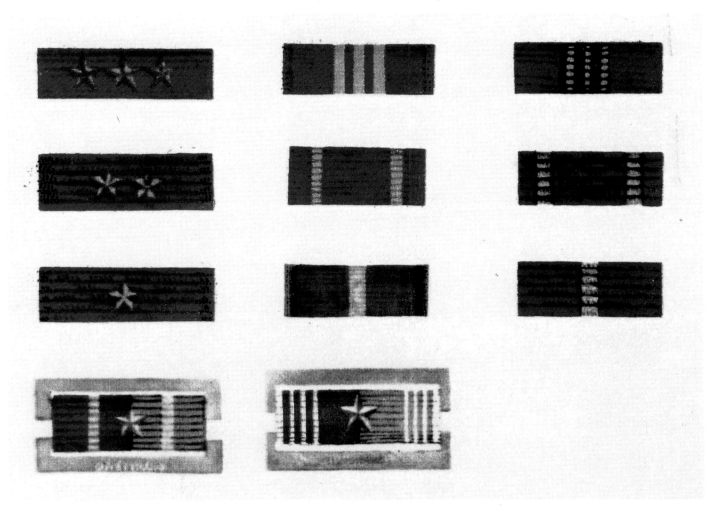

Service Ribbons: 1st Class (top row). 2nd Class (second row). 3rd Class (third and bottom rows).

Chapter 2
Obsolete Medals of the Socialist Republic of Vietnam and the National Liberation Front

Documented SRV battle flag 28" x 22" captured during the 1972 Nguyen Hue Spring Offensive.

1. Liberation Order

This Order underwent significant change in its design. The now obsolete Order closely resembles the current version of the Decoration.

Obsolete Liberation Order.

The Brass Fortress of the Fatherland Decoration.

2. Brass Fortress of the Fatherland

This previously high ranking Decoration (THANH-DONG TO-QUOC) of the SRV, which held precedence with the three other "Hero" Decorations (People's Armed Forces, Liberation Armed Forces and Labor) was generally worn centered on the left breast. It has mysteriously disappeared from the roster of official Orders and Decorations. It was bestowed for efforts in support of the resistance in the South in two classes. It is possible that this Decoration has been merged with an existing Order, such as the Brass Fortress Order (THANH-DONG). It is one of the more distinctive medals, with its red enameled center and has historically commanded high values, based on condition. Recent photos of PAVN veterans indicate continued display of this medal, but it has been moved to the right breast. Although not included in the list of official awards, many fine specimens are still being brought back from the Saigon markets.

3. PAVN Honor Medal

Awarded to families of those, who suffered hardships and death in Military Region 7 (Saigon), during the final phase of the Second Indochina War, this medal features the most prized field weapon of the War, the Chinese Type 56 Kalashnikov 7.62 mm AK-47 assault rifle and the SRV flag. The reverse is inscribed: HUY CHUONG DANH DU (Honor Decoration) and MIEN DONG GIAN LAO MA ANH DUNG (Heroes Who Suffered Adversity in Eastern Nambo). Nambo is a Vietnamese expression for the southern part of South Vietnam and portions of Laos and Cambodia, formerly known as Cochinchina.

This is a famous Vietnamese Communist quote and is included in one of the songs used by the VC to describe the beauty of the jungle. Anyone living in Vietnam after 1975, knows this quote.

PAVN Honor Medal.

Engraved Reverse of the PAVN Honor Medal.

4. Victory Decoration

This NLF Decoration is one of a series of four Decorations, of which only the Resolution for Victory Decoration is listed as an official award of the SRV. It was intended for award in two classes as denoted by the small stars on the hero style ribbon suspension bar. The planchet is inscribed CHIEN THANG (Victory).

NLF Victory Decoration.

NLF Oppose America Save Country Decoration.

5. Oppose American Save Country Decoration

The third in this series of NLF Decorations, this was also intended for award in two classes as denoted by the stars on the ribbon suspension bar. It is inscribed CHONG MY CUU NUOC (Oppose America Save Country).

6. Liberation Decoration

The last in this series, it was also intended for award in two classes. It is inscribed GIAI PHONG (Liberation). Although it has been speculated that this may have been an updated NLF version of the official SRV Liberation Decoration, this appears not to be the case based on the text of *Orders and Decorations*.

NLF Liberation Decoration.

Heroes Who Destroy Americans Decoration.

The NLF Hero Series (7 through 12)

7. Heroes Who Destroy Americans

This NLF Decoration was awarded in three classes, plus a special class for heroic actions in battle against American forces. It is the first in a series of NLF Decorations, which were liberally awarded to NLF units and combatants. It is inscribed DUNG-SI DIET MY (Valiant Soldier Destroy Americans) and like the other medals of this type, which follow, was worn on the right breast. Classes are denoted by CAP I, II or III on the planchet. A special class is inscribed UU-TU. Quotas for enemy KIA were established by the NLF, based on unit size, to determine the appropriate class to be awarded. The medal is suspended from a hero style metal bar. Sylvester notes the existence of an American made copy of this award.

NLF hero mining downed U.S. helicopter for valuable weapons, parts and ammunition, circa 1967. Courtesy of F.C. Brown.

8. Heroes Determined for Victory

Awarded to NLF forces for exemplary performance of duty, this medal was also bestowed in three classes (CAP I, II and III) and a special class (UU-TU). The planchet features two soldiers with weapons and the inscription DUNG-SI QUYET-THANG (Valiant Soldier Victory). It is suspended from a metallic hero style bar.

Heroes Determined for Victory Decoration.

Heroes Who Destroy Mechanized Equipment Decoration.

9. Heroes Who Destroy Mechanized Equipment

Awarded in one class to NLF forces for destroying tanks, armored personnel carriers (APC's) and other mechanized enemy vehicles. The inscription reads DUNG-SI DIET CO-GIOI (Valiant Soldier Destroy Mechanize). It too is suspended from a metal hero style bar. American made copies exist.

10. Heroes Who Destroy Communications

Awarded in one class to NLF personnel for destroying communications related equipment and/or facilities. The inscription reads: DUNG SI DANH GIAO THONG (Valiant Soldier Combat Communications). It is also suspended from a metal hero style bar.

Heroes Who Destroy Communications Decoration.

Heroes Who Destroy Aircraft Decoration.

11. Heroes Who Destroy Aircraft

Awarded in one class to NLF personnel who destroyed airplanes or helicopters. The inscription reads: DUNG-SI DIET MAY-BAY (Valiant Soldier Destroy Airplane). The suspension bar is also metal.

There are rumors that this award also exists with a helicopter in lieu of the falling jet aircraft. This confusion may stem from the Ap Bac Commemorative Badge, which features a falling helicopter. This decoration (see page 65) is extremely rare.

12. Valiant Soldier Assault

This is the last in this series of NLF Hero Decorations. It was awarded in a single class to personnel participating in an assault upon enemy positions. The inscription reads: DUNG-SI XUNG-KICH (Valiant Soldier Assault). It is suspended from a bi-color metallic bar.

Valiant Soldier Assault Decoration.

Heroes Determined for Victory Decoration.

13. Heroes Determined for Victory

A PAVN award in one class, the medal features the simple inscription: QUYET-THANG (Victory). It is suspended from a red metallic hero style bar.

14. International Duty

A PAVN award for service outside the country, it was liberally bestowed for service in Cambodia during the Third Indochina War.

The inscription reads: VI NGHIA VU QUOC TE (For Duty International). It is suspended from a solid red hero style metal bar.

PAVN International Duty Decoration.

PAVN Warrior to be Emulated Decoration 1960.

15.-16. Warrior to be Emulated

These pins were bestowed on personnel for superior performance and adherence to duty. The PAVN version features annual dates ranging from 1960 through 1982 (the time of major changes in uniform regulations). The NLF version features a star on the suspension bar and most likely replaced the cloth flower emulation awards of the early 60s. Both versions feature the inscription CHIEN-SI THI DUA (Soldier Emulation).

Ta Thi Kieu, also know as Myoi Li, Hero of the Liberation Front, wears cloth emulation award on her right. On her left, she wears the Liberation Exploit Order 3rd Class, a Ho Chi Minh pin and the NLF Party Badge. Ta Thi Kieu was a VC unit leader from Bentre Province, who led a number of successful raids on South Vietnamese Army Posts and Police Stations during the 1960s. Courtesy of F.C. Brown.

17. Defeat American Aggression

This is an earlier PAVN award for soldiers and militia who took part in armed conflict against Americans. The inscription reads: QUYET-TAM DANH-THANG GIAC MY XAM-LOC (Determined to Fight American Aggression). It is suspended from a solid red metal bar.

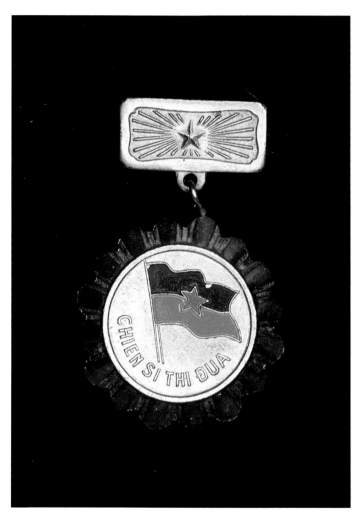

NLF Warrior to be Emulated Decoration.

PAVN Defeat American Aggression Decoration.

18. Unknown NLF Award

Although much speculation about this award exists, it is uncertain what purpose it served. The inscription GPQ MEIN NAM VN stands for the South Vietnam Liberation Army.

19. Emulation Award

This is a more formalized NLF emulation award, which has been observed in several configurations. It is most likely that the red/blue painted center was the creation of an inventive merchant intent on boosting sales of this otherwise unattractive medal. It has been observed suspended from both a hero style ribbon bar as well as an NLF blue and red pentagonal suspension ribbon. It is inscribed THI DUA (Emulation).

Unidentified NLF Decoration.

NLF Emulation Decoration.

Emulation Decoration with the center painted in NLF colors.

20. Volunteers for South Vietnam

This badge features a yellow, black and white hand, each holding a rifle, superimposed upon a segment of the globe. It is believed that this award was presented to foreign volunteers from the Communist world, who provided aid to the struggle in South Vietnam. It is inscribed: TINH NGUYEN SANG MEIN NAM VIET NAM (Volunteers Cross Over to South Vietnam).

Volunteers for South Vietnam Decoration.

Chapter 3
Commemorative Medals
and Campaign Badges

There are numerous commemorative and campaign badges of the Socialist Republic of Vietnam (SRV) and National Front for the Liberation of South Vietnam (NLF). They are usually found in the form of pinned badges, which are worn on the right breast. They generally commemorate important victories or war efforts. A sampling of a few of the more prominent badges are described in this chapter. The medal and commemorative badge for Ap Bac is discussed in Chapter VI.

Large Dien Bien Phu Order 1.25" diameter and small Dien Bien Phu Order 1" diameter. Small Order courtesy of Ned Broderick.

1.-3. Dien Bien Phu Order and Campaign Badge

Although described as an Order, this campaign badge (in two sizes), celebrates the Viet Minh victory over the French Colonial Forces in the battle of Dien Bien Phu in May, 1954. It was widely presented to those who participated in this famous battle. During the siege of Dien Bien Phu, which lasted for 55 days, the Viet Minh forces, under command of General Nguyen Van Giap, lost more than 8,000 men. The French Colonial Forces, consisting primarily of French, Vietnamese and Algerians, under the command of General Christian de Castries, lost 3,000 men during the siege. Of the 8,0000 French Colonial Force survivors another 50 percent died during the 60 day forced march to prison camps in the Red River Delta.

These badges are inscribed on the bottom: CHIEN SY DIEN-BIEN-PHU (Soldier of Dien Bien Phu). The SRV flag is inscribed below the gold star QUYET CHIEN/QUYET THANG (Decisive Battle/Resolved to Win). The top of the badge is inscribed XUAN (Spring) 1954. It is sometimes seen suspended from a metal hero style bar.

A distinct third version of the badge, which more closely resembles a classic campaign badge, features the SRV flag, with the inscription QUYET THANG (Resolved to Win) and the date of the Geneva Peace Conference "5-8," the day following the French surrender. It has also been observed being worn from a metal hero style suspension bar.*

A counter theory links this badge to the shooting down of Ensign Everett Alvarez on August 5, 1964. Ensign Alvarez became the fist American POW.

Dien Bien Phu Campaign Badge. Badge courtesy of Ned Broderick.

4. Operation Junction City Campaign (1967)

This badge commemorates the battles fought with U.S. and ARVN forces, which invaded Tay Ninh Province near the Cambodian border between February 22 and May 14, 1967 in a sweeping attempt to destroy VC bases and capture the headquarters of the Central Office for South Vietnam (COSVN). COSVN was the nerve center for all NLF action in the South. During the campaign the U.S. claimed 2,728 VC killed. U.S. losses numbered 282 killed, although Hanoi claimed 13,500 U.S. and ARVN killed in action. COSVN, which was not captured or destroyed, was forced to withdraw into Cambodia. The region, which was temporarily cleared of VC activity, was quickly re-infiltrated once the U.S. forces withdrew. The campaign badge reads: CHIEN THANG (Victory) and "U.S. Junction City" at the bottom. It was a rare find in the Saigon markets. Although it is in generally poor shape, its value lies in the fact that it is the only SRV or NLF badge which uses English.

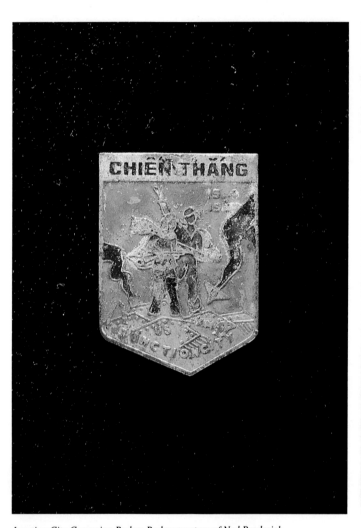

Junction City Campaign Badge. Badge courtesy of Ned Broderick.

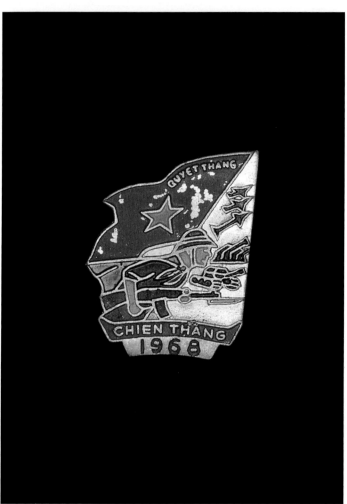

First Tet Offensive Campaign Badge.

5. First Tet Offensive, 1968

This badge was presented to those soldiers, who participated in the first Tet Offensive in 1968. The SRV flag is inscribed QUYET THANG (Resolved to Win) above the gold star and CHIEN THANG (Victory) 1968. This is an interesting concept, since it is a fact that the NLF suffered such heavy losses during the Tet Counteroffensive that the PAVN had to staff their units for the balance of the war against the Americans.

6. Nguyen Hue Offensive, 1972

Beginning in March 1972, PAVN Divisions 304 and 308, supported by armor invaded South Vietnam. Their target was the Provincial capital of Quang Tri. While this was occurring, the PAVN 324B moved on Hue. With assistance from elements of the 320B and 325C Divisions, the PAVN captured Quang Tri by early May. The South Vietnamese were able to hold to the north of Hue and by June, most of the captured areas had been liberated. PAVN losses totaled nearly 200,000 killed or captured, including more than 600 armored vehicles destroyed. This campaign marked the high water mark in the ARVN's performance and left the PAVN weakened and defeated. There would be no further PAVN general offensives until 1975.

1972 Nguyen Hue Campaign Badge.

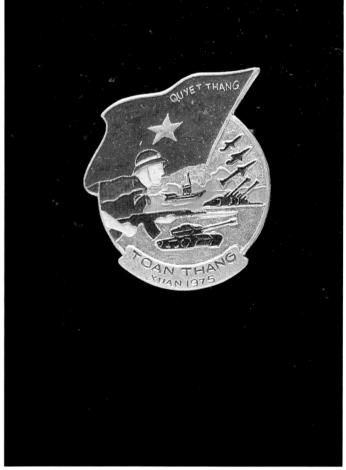

1975 Spring Offensive Campaign Badge.

7. 1975 Spring General Offensive

This campaign badge is for the early spring, 1975 Offensive, which preceded the Ho Chi Minh Offensive. It began on March 10, 1975 with an attack on Be Me Thout in the central highlands. PAVN forces were commanded by Senior General Van Tien Dung. It is inscribed TOAN THANG XUAN 1975 (Total Victory Spring, 1975). The SRV Flag reads: QUYET THANG (Resolved to Win).

PAVN ground forces and armor attack in Quang Tri Province during the Spring 1972 General Offensive. Courtesy of F.C. Brown.

8. Ho Chi Minh Campaign (1975)

During the first week of April, 1975, the PAVN committed more than 18 divisions with 300,000 men under the command of Senior General Van Tien Dung to the battle in South Vietnam. Saigon was assaulted from three sides. So fierce was the offensive that the ARVN crumbled in its wake. By April 30, 1975, T-54 tanks smashed through the Presidential Palace gates in Saigon and the Second Indochina War was over. The badge simply reads: CHIEN DICH HO CHI MINH (Ho Chi Minh Campaign).

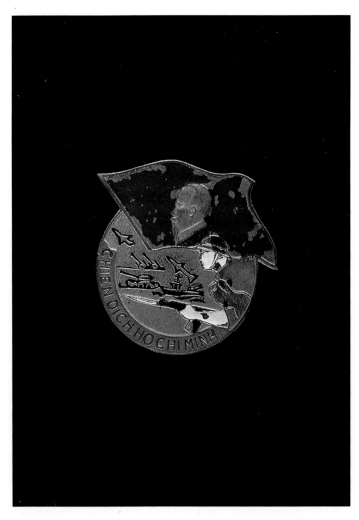

Ho Chi Minh Campaign Badge.

9. Spratly Island Campaign (1988)

Although the PAVN Navy traces its roots back to 1953, it has only been since the capture of the South Vietnamese fleet in 1975 and the addition of several Soviet built warships in 1978, that is has become a factor. Still, it pales in comparison to the Democratic Republic of China's Naval Fleet. The Spratly Islands (Quan Dao Thurong Xa), which are more than 450 miles southeast of Nha Trang, have been claimed by all of the nations bordering the South China Sea, including Borneo, Philippines, Indonesia, Malaysia and Taiwan. Vietnam and China, however seem to be the most willing to enter into armed conflict over them. It is suspected that the reason is rooted in the reputed oil reserves which lie in the vicinity of the Islands.

In 1975, when the Islands were being claimed by South Vietnam, the PAVN's naval infantry forces invaded them. In 1988, the SRV was severely repulsed by the Chinese Navy, which sank two Vietnamese ships operating in the Spratly Islands with a resulting loss of more than 70 Vietnamese lives. In 1992, China occupied at least one of the Spratly Islands. This campaign badge, issued to Naval personnel commemorates the 1988 battle. The metal suspension bar bears the acronym H.Q.N.D.V.N., or Hai-Quan Nhan-Dan Viet-nam (People's Navy of Vietnam). The planchet, which features the bust of a Vietnamese sailor reads CHIEN-SI TRUONG S.A. (Spratly Combatant).

Spratly Island Campaign Badge.

Air War Commemorative Badge.

10. Air War Commemorative

This badge commemorates the struggle against a major U.S. air offensive, Operation Linebacker. Launched against North Vietnam by the Americans, from May through late October, 1972. This offensive was an effort to both halt the flow of North Vietnamese supplies to the South, as well as to pressure the North to pursue a peaceful conclusion to the war in Paris. Over 150,000 tons of bombs had been dropped on the North by October 23, when the Operation was halted. It resumed again on December 19, in a further attempt to push the North to a settlement. During this 11 day period more

than 725 B-52 sorties were flown over North Vietnam. During this second phase, unofficially called Linebacker II, 15 of the B-52s were shot down by the North. Within nine days of its cessation on December 30, a cease-fire had been agreed to in principle. Twelve days later, it was signed by Henry Kissinger and North Vietnam's chief negotiator, Le Duc Tho.

The badge shows a fist in the colors of the SRV flag punching a U.S. Air Force B-52 out of the sky. It is inscribed: KY-NIEM CHIEN THANG (Remember Victory) 1972-1982.

11. 50th Anniversary of the New Woman

This gilt medal celebrates the 50th anniversary of the association of women who work for and defend the Fatherland. It is inscribed: NGUOI PHU MOI XAY DUNG BAO VE TO QUOC (Women Association Building Security for Fatherland). With Vietnam's long history of wars, women have played key roles in the PAVN, Communist Party and the industrial efforts of the country. Women have often been featured as heroines of both the military and industry and have received high awards, such as the Military Exploit Order and the Hero of Labor Decoration.

50th Anniversary of the New Woman Badge.

Special Forces 25th Anniversary Badge.

12. Special Forces (Sapper Branch) 25th Anniversary

This colorful medal celebrates the 25th anniversary of the PAVN's special forces, or Sapper Branch. Although the concept has roots in the 13th century, original PAVN attempts to establish special operation units date from the early 50s. In March 1967, the PAVN established the 305 Dac Cong, or Sapper Command with headquarters at Xuan Mai. On March 19, Ho Chi Minh visited their headquarters and this date is recognized as the founding date of the special forces. Sappers were initially deployed to counteract the impact of the American Long Range Reconnaissance Patrols (LURRP's). In 1969, an Underwater Warfare school was established at Long An and another Sapper Swimmer school at Kien Hoa.

In 1970, PAVN 11A and 11B Counter Reconnaissance Companies were deployed in South Vietnam. During the battle at Ban Me Thout in 1975, which lead to the eventual collapse of the South, the 198th Sapper Regiment spearheaded the attack.

Sapper Units now form a key part of the PAVN's overall operational strength. From the original 500 man Naval Sapper Group 126, which operated in the vicinity of the Cua Viet River, near the Demilitarized Zone (DMZ) during the Second Indochina War, the Naval Infantry (HAI-LUC CHIEN-DOI) was formed. It has grown into one of the largest marine corps in the world with more than 27,000 personnel serving in five brigades (126, 147, 148, 149 and 950).

The metal suspension bar is inscribed BIEN-CHUNG DAC CONG (Sapper Branch). The planchet bears the dates March 19, 1967-March 19, 1992 and the numeral 25 surrounding the Sapper branch insignia of a dagger above a satchel charge.

13. 10th Anniversary of Liberation of the Coastal Zones

This colorful metal badge and suspension bar was issued to commemorate the liberation of South Vietnam's coastal zones during the Spring 1975 Offensive. The suspension bar reads KY-NIEM 10 NAM GIAI PHONG (Remember 10 Years Liberation). The planchet is inscribed HUYEN HAI (Sea District).

Liberation of the Coastal Zones Commemorative.

Hanoi War Zone Commemorative Badge.

14. Hanoi War Zone

This gold-finished SRV badge commemorates the war in Hanoi. It is designed in hero style with a metal suspension that reads: KY NIEM (Remember). The planchet reads CK, an acronym for CHIEN KU (War Zone) and HANOI.

15. NLF An Ninh 15th Anniversary Medal

This medal commemorates the 15th year of the NLF An Ninh security forces which were formed in 1960. It reads BAN AN NINH MIEN NAM 1960-1975 (Security Section South Vietnam). The NLF was dismantled in 1975, shortly after the fall of Saigon.

NLF An Ninh Commemorative Medal.

Chapter 4
Political Badges

NLF Hero wearing Ho Chi Minh Pin above the Liberation Exploit Order 3rd Class and two Liberation War Exploit 3rd Class Orders. Courtesy of F.C. Brown.

These Communist Party badges are usually worn on the right breast by both military and civilian personnel unless noted other- wise. This chapter will review some of the more common badges based on frequency of observation.

1.-2. and 3. Ho Chi Minh Badges

The small gilt and larger, new, red enamel Ho Chi Minh badges are frequently observed on both military and civilian personnel. The third vintage Ho Chi Minh badge with red gilt is from an earlier period and quite rare. Chairman Ho was the spiritual leader of both the Party as well as the country. Even after his death in the fall of 1969, his inspiration continued to motivate the country. To this day, his memory is revered by the entire country. Saigon was renamed Ho Chi Minh City following the North's victory in 1975.

Small gilt Ho Chi Minh badge.

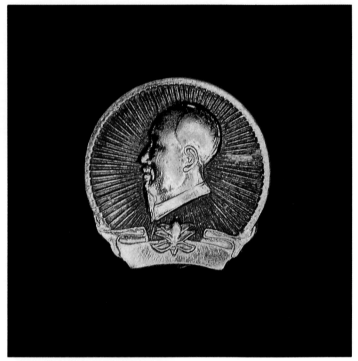

Common red enamel Ho Chi Minh badge.

Vintage red enamel Ho Chi Minh badge.
Badge courtesy of Ned Broderick.

4. Communist Party 40th Anniversary

Although extremely popular elsewhere in the Communist world, this is one of the rare usages of the hammer and sickle symbol observed on Vietnamese medals. The medal celebrates the 40th anniversary of the founding of the Vietnamese Communist Party in February, 1930. The hammer and sickle is superimposed on a red enamel center with the number "40" in red enamel below it. The medal is suspended from a solid red hero style ribbon bar. This is another of a select few SRV medals with a serial number engraved on its back.

Communist Party 40th Anniversary Decoration.

Original Communist Youth Group Badge. Badge courtesy of Ned Broderick.

5. Communist Youth Group Badge

The Communist Youth Group is the initial introduction to Party activities for young Vietnamese. Upon acceptance, they are issued this attractive enamel pin along with a 16 page, 3" x 4" document known as The Doan Vien, which details their identity and records their payment of party dues. The badge is inscribed: DOAN THANH NIEN CONG SAN HO CHI MINH (Ho Chi Minh Communist Youth Group). It was previously inscribed: DOAN THANH LAO DONG VIET-NAM (Vietnam Workers' Party Youth Group). The change was apparently made to commemorate the memory of Ho Chi Minh sometime after his death in 1969. DOAN VIEN translates as Certificate of Group Membership. Its value is greatly enhanced by its date of issue. The older the Doan Vien, the more valuable it is. The earlier badge reads: DOAN THANH NIEN NHAN DAN CACH MANG HO CHI MINH (People's Revoluntionary Ho Chi Minh Youth Group).

Current Communist Youth Group Badge.

Current Communist Youth Group membership book.

Communist Youth Group membership book identification pages.

6. National Liberation Front Badge

This small badge was often worn by NLF (VC) personnel, on the left breast (to the left of any Orders). It reads: MAT TRAN DAN TOC GIAI PHONG MIEN NAM VIET NAM (National Front for the Liberation of South Vietnam).

NLF Party Badge. Badge courtesy of Ned Broderick.

Vintage NLF Party Badge. Badge courtesy of Ned Broderick.

Vintage NLF Pin

This well worn pin dates from the early days of the Second Indochina War and reads THI DUA (Emulate), QUYET CHIEN (Resolved to Fight), QUYET THANG (Resolved to Win) and GIAC MY (Denounce America).

Vintage Ho Chi Minh Pin
This recent discovery features Ho Chi Minh and the SRV flag. It reads CHU TICH (Chairman) HO CHI MINH.

Vintage Ho Chi Minh Badge. Badge courtesy of Ned Broderick.

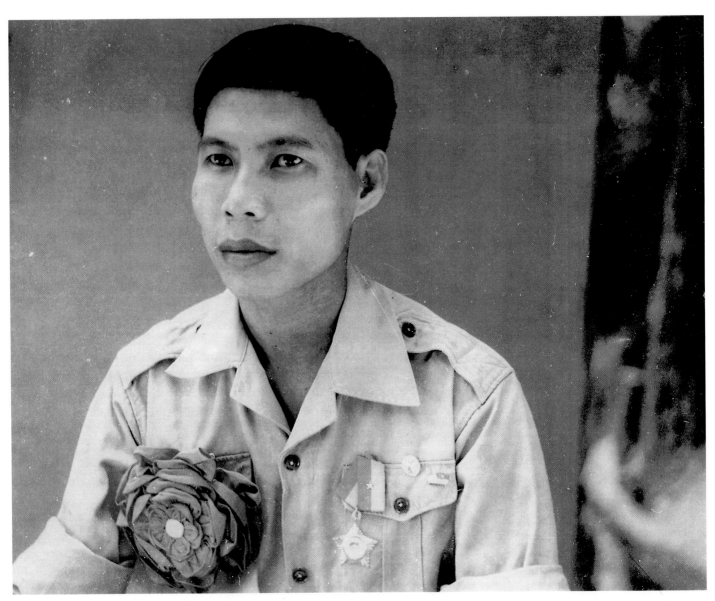

NLF Officer wearing his NLF Party Badge. He is also wearing the Liberation Exploit Order 3rd Class, a Ho Chi Minh pin, and a cloth emulation award circa 1965. Courtesy of F.C. Brown.

Chapter 5
Local and Cultural Awards

There are an infinite variety of these badges, with a wide variety of quality, ranging from intricately cast versions to simple, tin-like, "beer can" versions. A few are presented here as examples of the genre.

1. Ho Chi Minh City Medal

This is one of the better quality, more intricate examples of local awards. It has been observed suspended from both a metal hero style bar pictured here, as well as a variety of pentagonal suspension ribbons. The bar reads: THANH PHO HO CHI MINH (Ho Chi Minh City).

Ho Chi Minh City Medal.

2. Ho Chi Minh City Youth League
This is an example of a beer can or flat, stamped metal variety of local awards. It is extremely one dimensional in appearance. The metal suspension bar reads THANH PHO HO CHI MINH (Ho Chi Minh City). The planchet reads VIDANEM (Youth Group) on the red ribbon and DOAN THANH NIEM CONG SAN HO CHI MINH (Ho Chi Minh Communist Youth Group).

Ho Chi Minh City Youth League "beer can" Badge.

Byelorussian Friendship Badge.

3. White Russian Friendship Badge
This attractive, painted badge commemorates the friendship between White Russia (Byelorussia) and the Vietnamese people. The metal hero style suspension bar is inscribed: BINH TRI THIEN BELORUXIA (Good Friends Byelorussia). The planchet is inscribed NGUOI TOT VIEC TOT (Good People are Good Workers). It appears to be of rather recent vintage, dating back to the period of closer relationships with the Soviets.

4. Ho Chi Minh City 15th Anniversary Cultural Medal

This award honors the 15th anniversary of a Ho Chi Minh City cultural group. Although another example of an inexpensive, stamped, beer can medal, its vibrant colors set it apart from the traditional red and gilt of many of the SRV awards. It features a stylized dove, suspended between sky blue and ocean green on the hero style metal suspension bar. The planchet features a traditional dancer and the inscription T.P. (Thanh Pho) Ho Chi Minh (Ho Chi Minh City) and the number "15".

Ho Chi Minh City Cultural Badge.

Chapter 6

Ap Bac

Ap Bac Medal.

Ap Bac Medal with alternate ribbon.

NLF 261st Battalion Iron & Steel Squad at Ap Bac, circa 1963. Courtesy of NVVA Museum.

The battle of Ap Bac took place on January 2, 1963. It was a set piece battle pitting the Army of the Republic of Vietnam (ARVN) 7th Division against the 261st National Liberation Front Battalion. It took place in the rice paddies surrounding the crescent-shaped villages of Ap Tan Toi and Ap Bac, 30 miles southwest of Saigon.

It was intended to be a simple "mop up" operation of a VC radio company and its 120 man security company. The ARVN was led by General Huynh Van Cao, assisted by his American advisor, Army Lieutenant Colonel John Paul Vann. The plan was simple, about 600 ARVN troops, supported by armored personnel carriers (APC's) and Huey Cobra Gunships, would helicopter to the village in a pre-dawn surprise attack. Two additional ARVN airborne divisions were to be held in reserve in case the VC attempted to flee.

Things unraveled fast. Hampered by fog, the weakest link of the ARVN forces made initial contact with the well entrenched VC and were cut to ribbons in a wicked crossfire. As the battle continued to unfold, the VC burst from cover and attacked the APC's with hand held satchel charges.

Before the day ended, more than 80 ARVN and three American advisors were killed in action. Four helicopters, including one of the invincible Cobra Gunships, were shot down and an addi-tional 14 damaged by VC gun fire. Numerous APC's were left smoldering in the rice paddies, deserted by their ARVN crews, who were either killed or wounded.

By 10 pm, the VC, who would later be given the appellation "Iron and Steel Squad," disappeared into the night, returning to their base in Cambodia. Through interrogation of their commander, who was captured later during the war, it was learned that they had lost 18 cadre, although only three VC bodies were recovered at the scene.

In a bizarre twist, while ARVN forces were in the field the next morning picking up their dead, General Cao ordered a counterattack and started raining down artillery shells on his own men, killing another four. Colonel Vann's concise, if not politically correct, summation of the ARVN, "A miserable damn performance, just like always."

The politically astute NLF was quick to make heroes out of the 261st. A special unit medal, known simply as the Ap Bac Medal, was cast in their honor. There was also a commemorative (beer can) badge and a special unit "honor" flag created.

Unfortunately, the medal does not remain among those included as official awards of the SRV, most likely because in 1963 all re-

Ap Bac Honor Banner 45" x 30". Banner courtesy of Ned Broderick.

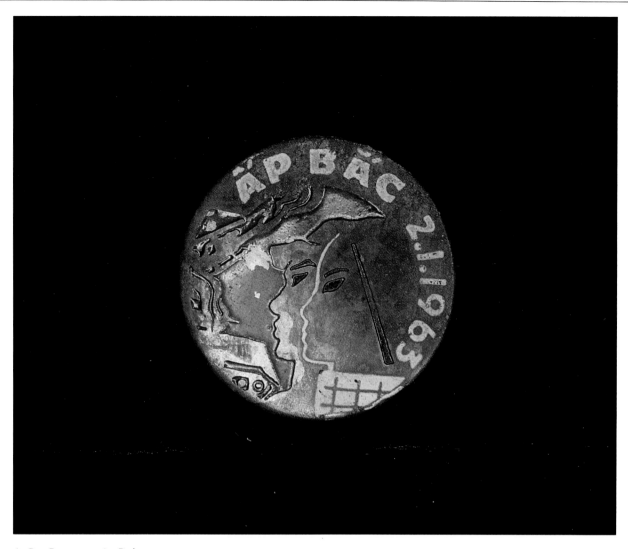

Ap Bac Commemorative Badge.

cipients were NLF personnel. The planchet itself, although readily available in Saigon markets, has never been positively associated with either a pentagonal suspension ribbon, or a hero style metal or ribbon bar. It is pictured here with two alternative pentagonal suspension ribbons, commonly associated with NLF medals of the same era. Neither, however may be the correct combination. The planchet, which is in the form of a stylized gold star is inscribed, "Ap Bac 2.1.1963" (January 2, 1963). It features the profile of a male and female VC fighter on the right side and a burning helicopter and APC on its left side.

The commemorative pin is of the flat, beer can style and is painted. It features the same design as the medal, but with color added. It is less common.

The unit honor flag, which is as valuable as it is ornate, features the official SRV Decoration of Victory in its center. Above the Decoration reads: "Ground Force Military Heroes for Liberation of South Vietnam." Below the Decoration reads: "Ground Force Military Heroes of Cai Lay and My Tho;" "Determined to Oppose America and Diem" and "Victory at Ap Bac January 2, 1963."

Chapter 7
Cap Badges

The Socialist Republic of Vietnam (and for a time the National Liberation Front) is noted for the proliferation of military and paramilitary units. Each of these various groups at one time or another had their own distinctive cap badges, most of which are fitted for the pith or sun helmet favored as headgear by both military personnel as well as civilians. In some cases, the badges are fitted with a simple wire pin back for use on the cloth "boonie" cap. These cap badges can provide the collector with yet another avenue to pursue.

Among the most prevalent cap badges are the following:

Captured NLF Battle Flag, circa 1967.

I. PAVN Badges

1. PAVN Army (Luc-Quan)

This is one of the toughest, battle hardened forces in all of Southeast Asia. The Army has been the victor in all three Indochina Wars. The cap badge features a raised gold star on red enamel background surrounded by shocks of rice over a toothed gear wheel. Prior to 1958, it was worn only by officers. During the early years of the Second Indochina War, PAVN forces would remove these cap badges before crossing into the South in an effort to disguise their true identity. Since the major revision in uniform regulations in 1982, the red PAVN cap badge has been worn by all ranks of all branches (except certain Cong An personnel, as noted below).

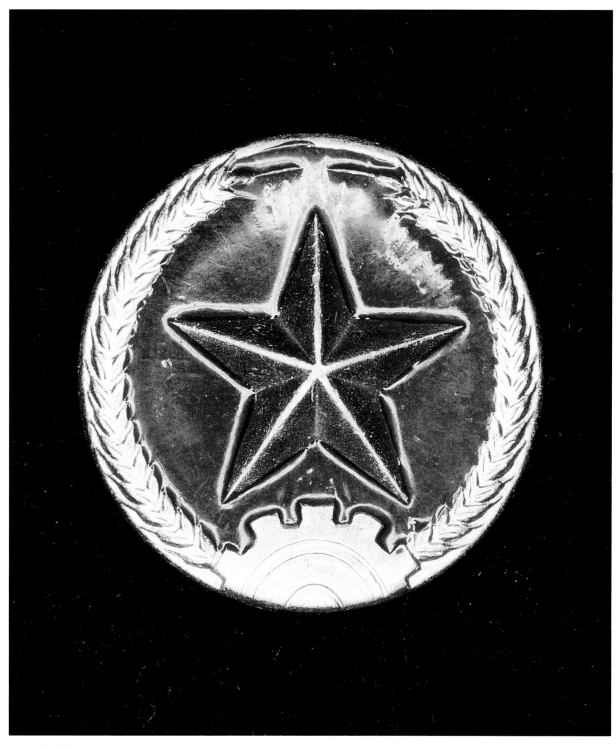

Current PAVN Badge.

2. PAVN Army, Field & General Grade Officer's Peaked Cap Badges

Consisting of the standard PAVN circular badge, as described above, this peaked cap badge is surrounded by two gold pine branches for General Officers and two silver pine branches for Field Grade Officers.

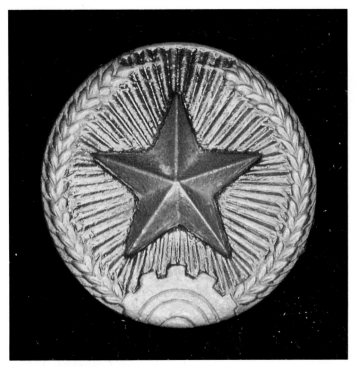

PAVN General Officer's Badge.

Vintage PAVN Badge. Badge courtesy of Ned Broderick.

PAVN Field Grade Officer's Badge.

3. PAVN Navy (Hai-Quan)

Growing from an original 500 man PAVN coastal defense detachment in 1953, the Navy had grown to 2,500 by 1964, but was still not a major factor during the Second Indochina War. Not until the capture of more than 1,300 South Vietnamese vessels did the Navy become an important component of the SRV's overall military forces. Its headquarters is located in Hanoi. It documents its founding as having occurred on April 5, 1964, the second night of the Gulf of Tonkin incident.

These pre-1982 cap badges, which date from the early 70s closely parallel those of the Army, with the gold star superimposed over a red enamel anchor. Also pictured is an earlier version with the anchor in gilt. The background was changed from Army red to dark blue.

Navy Badge with gilt anchor. Badge courtesy of Ned Broderick.

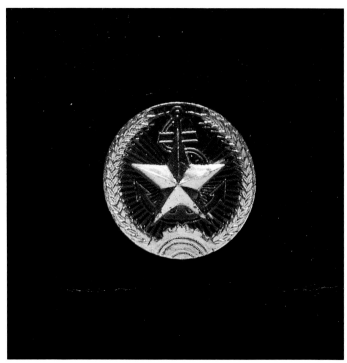

Navy Badge with red anchor.

4. Air Force (Khong-Quan)

Like the Naval forces, the Air Force originated from within PAVN. Original pilot training came from the Chinese and Soviet Air Force. Although, they possessed both MIG-17s and MIG-21s, the Air Force also was not a major factor during the Second Indochina War. Air Force Headquarters is located at the former French air base at Bac Mai.

The pre-1982 cap badge, adopted in 1965, mirrored the PAVN badge with the gold star superimposed over silver wings. The background was sky blue. Earlier versions worn by officers, dating from the late 1950s and mid-1960s, have the wings superimposed over a red background and a silver gray background, respectively.

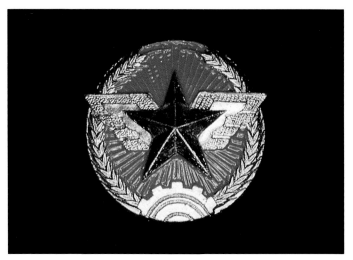

Pre-1982 Air Force Badge.

Vintage Air Force Badge, circa 1960. Badge courtesy of Ned Broderick.

Vintage Air Force Badge, circa late 1950s. Badge courtesy of Ned Broderick.

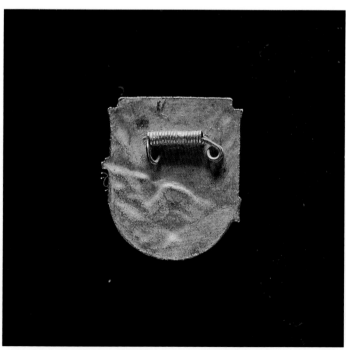

Border Guard Badge. Badge courtesy of Ned Broderick.

Border Guard Badge Reverse. Badge courtesy of Ned Broderick.

II. Security Forces

1. Cong An

Vietnam's first security force, the People's Armed Public Security Force (CONG AN NHAN DAN VO TRANG), was formed in 1950. A small badge was issued in 1957 to members of the Cong An Nhan Dan Vo Trang. It reads: CHIEN SI GIOI (Border Soldier). It had an unusual spring mounted back in lieu of the usual bent pin device. The weapon is a Chinese made, Soviet model, 9mm PPsh41 submachine gun with a 31 round magazine.

In 1959, it was dissolved and replaced by the Cong An, which was controlled by the Political General Directorate and grew to include nearly 25,000 personnel by 1964. It was tasked with providing border and coastal security. It also provided military prison guards during the Second Indochina War.

In 1979, the Cong An was renamed the Border Defense Force and control of all, but a few select units, was transferred to the Military General Staff Directorate. Its current strength is estimated at 60,000. Its prominence grew dramatically following a strong performance during the 1979 border clashes with the People's Republic of China. Cong An units also played key roles during the Third Indochina War in Cambodia.

The Cong An badge is also modeled after the PAVN badge, but has a deep green surround and the legend CA superimposed on the gear wheel at the bottom. It was originally worn by all members of the Cong An, but since 1979, it is worn only by select Ministry of Interior police and paramilitary units. Since 1979, BDF members wear the standard red enamel PAVN cap badge.

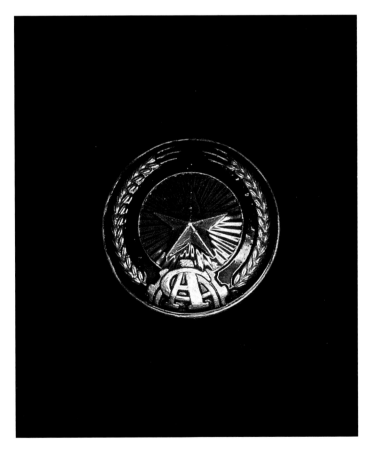

Cong An Badge.

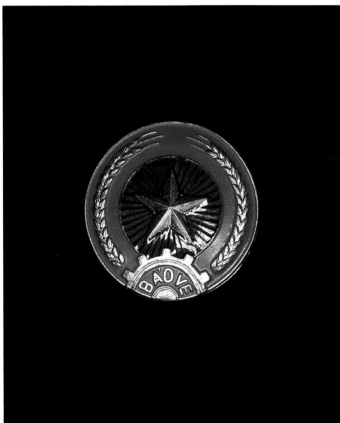

Bao Ve vintage Badge.

2. Bao Ve

Formed in 1960, the Bao Ve were charged with the security of Vietnam's military units and military prisons. They served under the PAVN's Political General Directorate (TONG CUC CHINH TRI). The Bao Ve monitored compliance with military regulations and the country's laws. Their authority extended to civilians in matters involving military personnel. Their original cap badge had a blue surround with BAOVE inscribed within the toothed gear wheel. A more current badge replaced the blue surround with gold. The Bao Ve were disbanded in 1980 and their role was assumed by Cong An units.

Bao Ve Badge.

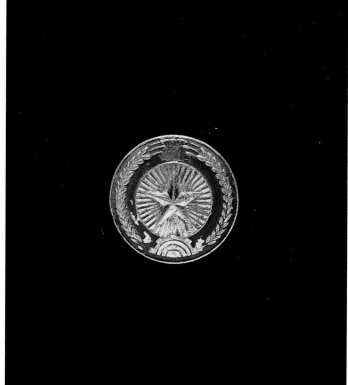

Vintage PAVN An Ninh Badge. Badge courtesy of Ned Broderick.

3. An Ninh

Also formed in 1960, An Ninh units serve as the PAVN's military police forces. In 1980, they took over from the Bao Ve units as the guardians of Vietnam's military prisons.

Three An Ninh badges are known to exist. First, is the original version with green surrounding a gilt center and star. A barely visible "AN" is stamped into the reverse. Only the green surround identifies the wearer as a security personnel. A second pre-1982 version has brilliant blue surrounding a red enamel center and gilt star. The "AN" is clearly visible at the bottom. The last is an obsolete NLF version for their own An Ninh personnel. Again, the AN is clearly visible at the bottom.

PAVN An Ninh units were the only security forces encountered south of the 17th parallel (Demilitarized Zone) during the Second Indochina War.

Pre-1982 PAVN An Ninh Badge.

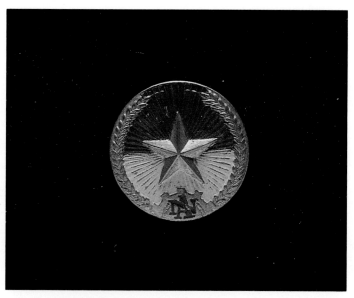

NLF An Ninh Badge. Badge courtesy of Ned Broderick.

III. Special Units

1. *Armed Youth Assault Force*

The Armed Youth Assault Force, or THANH NIEN XUNG PHONG (TNXP) is a paramilitary force based primarily in the southern part of the country. It existed in the NLF's liberated areas as early as 1972. To avoid creating a potentially counterrevolutionary force of NLF veterans in the South, Hanoi tapped the youth to staff these paramilitary units. The TNXP's strength is estimated between 1.5 and 2 million. Their units were used extensively during the Third Indochina War and apparently acquitted themselves well in battle in Cambodia.

Their cap badge, while smaller than that of the PAVN, bears the distinctive acronym, TNXP, at the bottom.

Armed Assault Youth Force Badge.

Special Air Unit Badge.

2. *Special Air Unit (KDDV)*

This rather large, special unit badge, designed for wear on a sun helmet, unfortunately, remains unidentified. The KDDV most likely stands for Khong-Doan Don-Vi (air mobile (medical) unit). Conversations about this badge with a Vietnamese diplomat, who was a former Dac Cong Sapper, failed to result in a positive identification of the badge. The wings and cross definitely link it to an air mobile unit with a medical mission. It dates from 1982, based on its usage of components from the current PAVN branch insignia.

3. Special Navy Unit

This oversized Navy badge (HAI QUAN) features a crossed anchor and key and was most likely worn by a Navy logistical support or supply unit. It features design components pre-dating the 1982 uniform changes.

Special Navy Unit Badge.

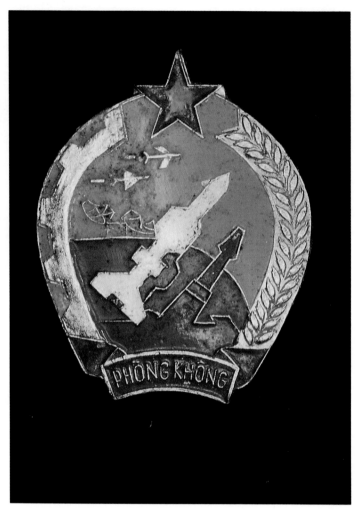

Air Defense Unit Badge. Badge courtesy of Ned Broderick.

4. Air Defense

This badge was designed for wear on a cloth cap by northern air defense units. The inscription reads: PHONG KHONG (Air Defense).

IV. National Liberation Front (Viet Cong)

Now obsolete, with all pretense of a separate political and military movement having been dropped at the end of the Second Indochina War, the NLF or Viet Cong cap badges were modeled after the PAVN's cap badge, but utilized the NLF's red and blue colors. Construction, however, is very simple with no raised features.

NLF Badges from 1973 (l.) and early 1960s (r.). Early 1960s Badge courtesy of Ned Broderick.

Meeting of NLF outstanding soldiers in April, 1965. Early version of the NLF Badge is displayed at the top of the stage. In attendance was Nyguen Huu Tho, President of the NLF in white shirt center; Nyguen Thi Dinh, Assistant Supreme Commander of the NLF, who was later revealed to be the only female PAVN Lieutenant General (standing), and Ta Thi Kieu (seated in black pajamas). Courtesy of F.C. Brown.

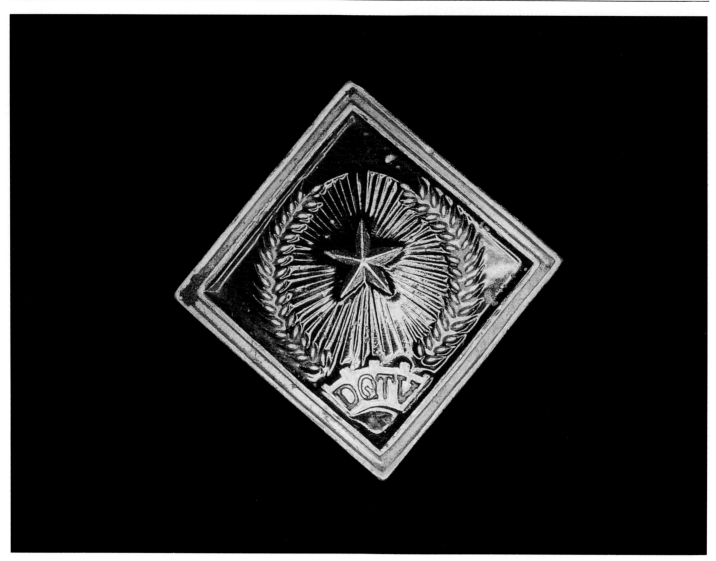

Civilian Militia Badge.

V. Civilian Militia

This cap badge is worn on a soft cap by members of the Self Defense Militia (DAN QUAN TU VE). The DQTV is the lowest tier of the PAVN's paramilitary forces. Numbering approximately 1 million members, the DQTV is lightly armed and operates on a country wide basis at the district and village level.

The Pith Helmet
Much mention has been made of the popular pith or sun helmet. These helmets are a collectible item of militaria unto themselves. They were the only piece of military gear actually manufactured in North Vietnam during the Second Indochina War.

NLF Officer wearing plastic pith helmet and cloth emulation award on left breast, circa 1965. Courtesy of F.C. Brown.

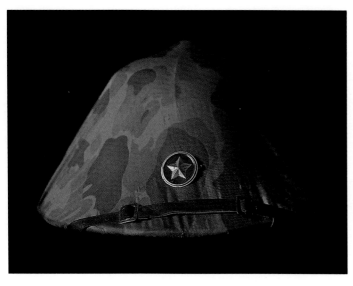

Early Viet Minh helmet with camouflage cover. Helmet courtesy of Ned Broderick.

PAVN An Ninh helmet. Helmet courtesy of Ned Broderick.

NLF An Ninh helmet. Helmet courtesy of Ned Broderick.

Chapter 8

Presentation Boxes

Presentation boxes run the gamut from fine hand lacquered wood to simple cardboard.

1. Lacquered Wood Box

The three most prestigious SRV orders, the Gold Star Order, the Ho Chi Minh Order and the Independence Order, have been presented to recipients in fitted, brown wood lacquered boxes with a gold decal of the National coat of arms (often observed affixed crooked) on the cover of the box. Given the nature of these senior awards, it seems fitting that such fine boxes are utilized. This style of presentation box is considered quite rare (as are the awards with which it has been associated). The top is not hinged to the bottom.

Lacquered wood presentation box with Gold Star Order. Photo courtesy of Peter Aitken.

Lacquered wood presentation box with Independence Order. Photo courtesy of Peter Aitken.

2. Polished Cotton Box

The Friendship Decoration (HUY CHOUNG HUU NGHI) is presented in this red polished cotton box with the center fitted for the award. Since this is an award presented to foreign recipients, it seems appropriate that the presentation box should be more stylish. The top is hinged to the bottom.

Polished cotton presentation box. Box courtesy of Ned Broderick.

Polished cotton presentation box fitted for Friendship Decoration. Box courtesy of Ned Broderick.

3. Plastic Box

This seems to be the most common form of presentation box. These boxes are observed in a variety of sizes. The inside is filled with red polished cotton, but it is not fitted to the medal, itself. The top of the box is clear plastic and lifts completely off the bottom, i.e. it is not hinged.

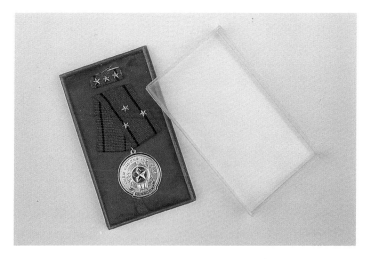

Red plastic presentation box with Labor Order and Service Ribbon. Photo courtesy of Peter Aitken.

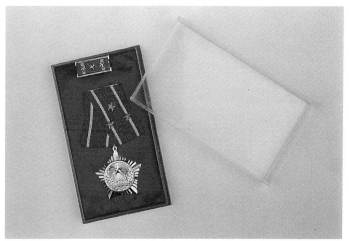

Red plastic presentation box with Resistance Order and Service Ribbon. Photo courtesy of Peter Aitken.

4. Cardboard Box

Apparently used for low level awards, such as longevity medals, this represents the simplest in SRV presentation boxes. The top is connected to the bottom.

Common red cardboard presentation box. Box courtesy of Ned Broderick.

Chapter 9
Award Documents

The award documents of the Socialist Republic of Vietnam and the National Front for the Liberation of South Vietnam are quite colorful. They feature the respective national flags and colorful borders. Size varies from large (11" x 14") to very small I.D. card size (3" x 5"). In the case of the I.D. card style document, space is typically provided on the reverse for notation of subsequent awards.

Examples of award documents in Cambodian and Laotian also exist for NLF awards to ethnic minority members. In addition to the documents bestowing Orders (HUAN CHUONG) and Decorations (HUY CHUONG), the SRV and NLF also issued colorful documents such as letters of attestation (GIAY CHUNG NHAN), letters of appreciation (GIAY KHEN) and letters of commendation (BANG KHEN). Entries were typically handwritten in flowing script and customarily stamped with round, red official seals. As noted by F.C. Brown, paper quality varies greatly. In many cases, these documents are frayed and torn, reflecting not only the poor quality of paper on which they were prepared, but also the conditions under which they were kept. They must be handled gently as they have a tendency to crumble. Value is established by age (date of issue), quality and condition. Documents for award of the more senior medals (Gold Star, Ho Chi Minh and the Independence Orders) or documents issued to identifiable parties, such as one of the Senior Generals (DAI TUONG) command higher values, regardless of their aforementioned condition.

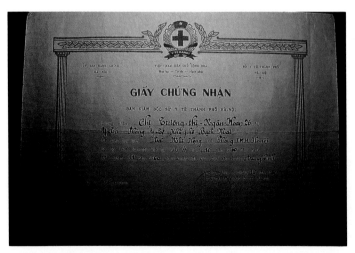

SRV 9" x 13" Attestation of Commendation. Certificate courtesy of Ned Broderick.

SRV 11" x 14" Letter of Appreciation. Certificate courtesy of Ned Broderick.

NLF Officer at award presentation ceremony, circa 1967. He is wearing the Liberation War Exploit Order 3rd Class on his left breast and a cloth emulation award on the right. Courtesy of F.C. Brown.

SRV 8" x 10" Letter of Appreciation. Certificate courtesy of Ned Broderick.

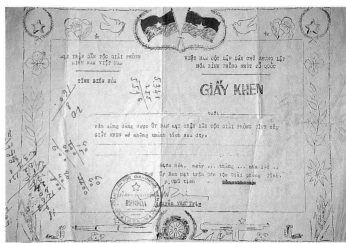

NLF 8" x 10" Letter of Appreciation. Certificate courtesy of Ned Broderick.

NLF 5" x 7" Letter of Appreciation.

SRV 11" x 14" Letter of Commendation. Certificate courtesy of Ned Broderick.

Award document for the Gold Star Order. Photo courtesy of Peter Aitken.

Award document for the Ho Chi Minh Order. Photo courtesy of Peter Aitken.

Award document for the Independence Order. Photo courtesy of Peter Aitken.

Award document for the Labor Order. Photo courtesy of Peter Aitken.

Award document for the Resistance Order. Photo courtesy of Peter Aitken.

Chapter 10

Miscellaneous

In May, 1977 the Third Indochina War started when the PAVN invaded Kampuchea in an effort to remove the fanatical and troublesome Khmer Rourge. After nearly two years of fighting, Phnom Penh was in PAVN hands and a puppet Cambodian government was established. The war, however, would continue on for another 10 years with PAVN forces remaining involved until the fall of 1989.

During this period, the puppet government bestowed many awards on its PAVN benefactors. One of the primary Kampuchean People's Republic (KPR) awards given to PAVN forces was their Friendship Decoration. This colorful award is commonly encountered by collectors and visitors to Vietnam. It is documented here to distinguish it from the SRV Friendship awards.

Another extraneous item for Red Cross collectible enthusiasts, is the Vietnamese Red Cross badge, which dates from 1953. HONG THAP-TU translates simply as Red Cross.

Additional miscellaneous badges are also presented here.

KPR Friendship Decoration and Service Ribbon.

1953 Red Cross Badge serial #1063. Badge courtesy of Ned Broderick.

Cycle of Nam by Joseph Metz. Courtesy of NVVA Museum.

Creative Labor Badge (LAO DONG SANG TAO).

Hanoi School Badge.

Women's Liberation Association Badge (LEIN HIEP PHU NU GIAI PHONG).

PAVN Heroes Who Protect Country Badge (DUNG SI GIU NUOC).

Family Contribution (of soldiers) Badge (GIA DINH QUAN NHAN).

Well behaved nephew's of Uncle Ho's soldiers of Dien Bien Phu Commemorative Badge.

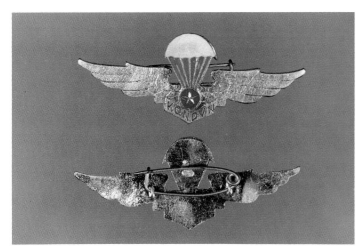

SRV Parachute Wings. Photo courtesy of George Petersen.

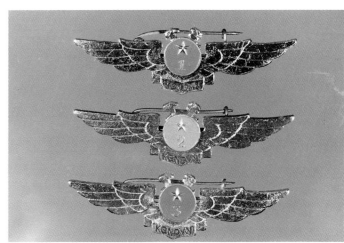

PAVN Air Force Pilot's Wings (1st, 2nd and 3rd class). Photo courtesy of George Petersen.

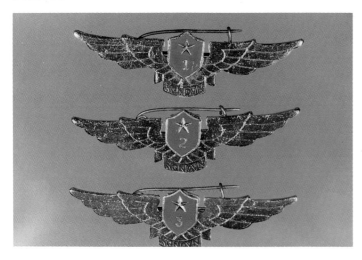

PAVN Air Crew Wings (1st, 2nd and 3rd class). Photo courtesy of George Petersen.

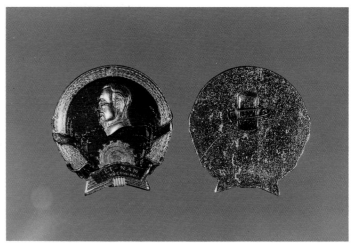

Large Ho Chi Minh Badge awarded to PAVN Fighter pilots for air-to-air kills. It is worn on the left breast. It has also been observed being worn by at least one NLF officer.

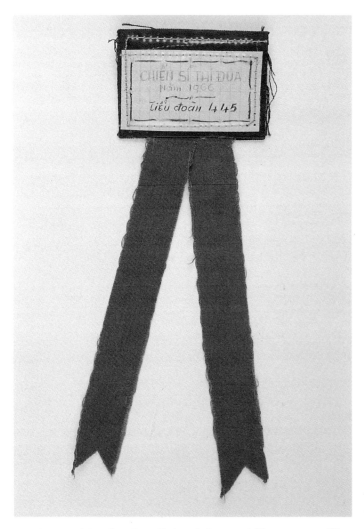

Viet Cong D445 Battalion (Long Tan) emulation award. Photo courtesy of Peter Aitken.

Medical Personnel (Quan Y) Badge.

Xuan Loc District Congress Badge.

50 Years of Resistance Commemorative Medal.

Hero Nguyen Van Troi Badge. Van Troi was executed by Saigon police after a failed attempt to assassinate Secretary of Defense Robert MacNamara in 1964. Although rejected for membership by the NLF earlier, the enemy astutely adopted him as a martyr following his execution.

Ho Chi Minh Badge worn on right breast.

Rare Ho Chi Minh Commemorative Medal. Doubt exists about the accuracy of the pentagonal ribbon pictured.

Career Education Badge.

Liberation Students Association Badge.

Ho Chi Minh City Medical School Badge.

Remember Resistance Badge.

Preparedness Badge.

Bentre Progressive Youth Badge.

Ho Chi Minh Badge.

Ho Chi Minh City Badge.

Liberation Youth Badge.

Young Soldier of Glory (Nguyen Van Troi) Badge.

20 Years of Cooperative Farming at Phu Son Badge.

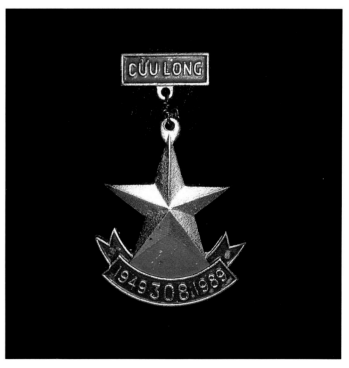

308 Division Commemorative Medal.

Assault Youth Commemorative Medal.

Unusual Hanoi-Hue-Saigon Badge with NLF and SRV Flags, in unfortunately poor condition. Badge courtesy of Ned Broderick.

Ho Chi Minh Badge.

Ho Chi Minh Youth Badge (1982).

Various Progressive (Revolutionary) Youth Badges.

Appendix:
Value Guide
SRV Orders and Decorations (Frequency of Presentation)

Page	Position	Value	Page	Position	Value	Page	Position	Value
7		E	45		B	79	L	E
8	T	D	46	L	C	79	R	E
8	B	E	46	R	B	80	L	B
10	L	C	47	L	B	80	R	B
10	R	C	47	R	B	81	TL	C
11	L	C	48	B	B	81	TR	C
11	R	C	49	L	C	81	B	A
13	L	C	49	R	B	82	L	B
13	R	D	50	L	A	82	R	B
14	L	B	50	R	B	84	TL	B
14	R	B	51	L	A	84	TR	B
15	L	B	51	R	B	84	CL	B
15	R	B	52		B	84	CR	B
17	L	B	54	TL	B	84	BL	C
17	R	B	54	TR	B	84	BR	C
18	L	B	54	B	C	85	TL	C
18	R	B	55	R	B	85	TR	B
19	L	B	55	L	B	85	B	C
21	L	C	56	TL	B	86	L	B
21	R	D	56	TR	B	86	R	C
22	L	D	57	L	B	88	TL	A
22	R	F	57	R	B	88	TR	A
23	L	C	58	T	B	88	BL	A
23	R	B	59		B	88	BR	A
24	T	B	60	L	A	89	TL	A
24	BL	B	60	R	B	89	TR	A
24	BR	B	61		A	89	BL	C
25	L	B	62		A	89	BR	C
25	R	B	64		F			
26	L	B	65		B	90	TL	C
26	R	B	66		D	90	TR	C
27	L	B	67		A	90	CR	B
27	R	B	68	TL	B	90	BL	E
30		D	68	TR	B	90	BR	A
31	L	B	68	B	B	91	TL	A
31	R	C	69	TL	B	91	TR	B
32		B	69	TR	B	91	BL	B
33	L	A	69	B	B	91	BR	C
33	R	A	70	TL	B	92	TL	A
34	L	A	70	TR	B	92	TR	A
34	R	B	70	B	C	92	CL	A
36	L	B	71	L	B	92	CR	A
36	R	B	71	R	B	92	BL	A
37	L	B	72	TL	B	92	BR	A
37	R	C	72	TR	B	93	TL	B
38	L	B	72	BL	B	93	TR	A
38	R	B	72	BR	B	93	CL	A
39	L	A	73	L	B	93	CR	B
39	R	C	73	R	C	93	BL	B
41	L	B	74	L	B	93	BR	C
41	R	B	74	R	B	94	TL	B
42	L	B	75	TL	B	94	TR	C
42	R	B	75	TR	B	94	BL	B
43	T	B	76		B	94	BR	B
43	B	B	78	TL	C	95	TL	A
44	L	B	78	TR	C	95	TR	A
44	R	B	78	B	C	95	B	A

Legend

Values		Positon	
A	Up to $50.00	T	= top of page
B	$51.00 to $100.00	B	= bottom of page
C	$101.00 to $250.00	R	= right side of page
D	$251.00 to $500.00	L	= left side of page
E	$501.00 to $1,000.00		
F	In excess of $1,000.00		

SRV Orders and Decorations
Frequency of Presentation

The following chart summarizes the award of the more senior SRV Orders and Decorations through the end of 1995:

MEDAL	NUMBER AWARDED
LABOR HERO DECORATION	12
GOLD STAR ORDER	16
HO CHI MINH	144
INDEPENDENCE ORDER	538
PEOPLE'S ARMED FORCES HERO	955
MILITARY EXPLOIT ORDER	1,627
FATHERLAND COMMEMORATIVE	2,795*

In other cases awards of some Orders and Decorations have ranged into the hundreds of thousands. As recorded by John Sylvester, Jr. in his Monograph, based on a statistical compilation released by the SRV, the following totals were awarded through April 1976:

MEDAL	NUMBER AWARDED
SOLDIER OF GLORY ORDER	517,533
VICTORY DECORATION	388,800
RESISTANCE DECORATION	360,793
VICTORY ORDER	121,501
COMBATANT ORDER	115,827
SOLDIER OF GLORY DECORATION	108,675
RESISTANCE ORDER	72,488

Note: The Fatherland Commemorative was only awarded to those Viet Minh forces, who served during the August 1945 Revolution, when they attempted to seize power from the defeated Japanese and their Vichy French allies.